PEOPLE PROJECTS and CHANGE

PRACTICAL TOOLS FOR MANAGING CHANGE PROJECTS

D1643052

PEOPLE PROJECTS and CHANGE

PRACTICAL TOOLS FOR MANAGING CHANGE PROJECTS

PAT PEGG JONES
SIMON STANDISH

Premium Publishing

Published by
Premium Publishing
27 Bassein Park Road,
London
W12 9RW
crestanorris@btconnect.com

First published 2006

ISBN 0-9550411-2-0

Design by Loman Street Studio
Photography by Stuart Wood

A catalogue record for this book is available from
the British Library

Contents

Co-authoring shares some features with project work. You bring to a finite task all of your experience and learning; the work demands help from people over whom you have no control; and in each stage of the work what you know, what you write, and what you understand about yourself are all expanded.

In the act of writing, past encounters were inevitably recalled of individuals who handled their role in a project in such a manner that it could be seen that there *is* an art in *setting up for success*. They demonstrated too that this capability has little to do with hierarchical status.

I want in particular to thank those who consciously contributed to our efforts. Clive Thompson for advice based on a distinguished career in private and public service; Joe Foley, whose wit, wisdom and vision mean I always leave a conversation richer in mind and spirit; Peter Block for his personal encouragement and from whom I continue to learn; Paul Burns supported me in this endeavour as graciously as others in the past; and Charlie Fields, who shared the benefit of his thinking and his creativity. Nigel Barnes was generous with his knowledge of project management and his experience of implementing a model. I am especially grateful for Alan Jones who in all he does, integrates the artist, the scientist, and the engineer. Jill Janov, Pat Kennedy and Diane Winstanley read early versions of the book – their detailed comments influenced my thinking as much as my words. And of course, my co-author Simon Standish.

Whilst stating personal thanks, I take responsibility for the shortcomings in how their contributions are reflected in this book.

P. Pegg Jones
April 2006

Co-authoring this book has provided me with a rare opportunity to reflect properly on the learning I derived from working with many talented colleagues and visionary clients. From the world of consulting I would particularly like to thank colleagues within the UMC group at Price Waterhouse for the opportunities to work along side them to formalise approaches to project management training and development. My time at Kinsley Lord was invaluable for developing a view on change management. I have been blessed with some great clients who each had fantastic ambitions for their organisations and were prepared to experiment and move with different approaches. I would like to particularly mention John Boyington, Peter Coe, Kevin Barton, Adrian Eddleston, Stephen Langford, Janet McMillan, Elaine Murphy, Julian Nettel, Claire Perry, Martin Roberts and Mary Wells for the opportunity to work on some really enjoyable and ground breaking projects. David Mathew and John Lockett are two very close friends and colleagues who have been very supportive of my efforts and have, over the years, provided some very wise counsel. Finally my thanks to Debbie, my wife, who has not only put up with the stresses and strains of my working life but also because of her training and consulting, has enriched my insight into the more personal issues of change and transitions. And Pat – thanks to you too! Co-authoring is not easy but I think we got the best bits from each other!

Simon Standish
April 2006

Introduction

Projects are becoming a way of life for people at work. As a methodology for getting things done, formal project management is taking root in more and more organisations. Forty years ago, big, risky, defence and construction projects spurred the development of more rigorous planning and control methodologies. Over the past 20 years, information systems and technology have extended the discipline. These kinds of projects fit well with the notions of teamwork to achieve delivery of specified products to time, cost and quality. The image of a project manager was of a professional with a commercial and engineering mentality and discipline, who finds it second nature to apply logic and linear thinking to plan, organise and control work. Now, the discipline of project management is being applied to a greater range of work such as the development of strategy and policy, new product and service development, and organisational change. It is also being take up by those with much broader backgrounds.

However many organisations seem slow to embrace the disciplines of project management to secure delivery. This may be down to culture, and the prevailing mentalities and skills of those in senior positions. At one extreme, work is defined in project terms and a project leader appointed, while the conventions of project management are ignored. Another extreme is the organisation where even the mention of project management raises immediate rejection.

In part, project management is the source of its own bad press. To many, project management brings to mind interminable levels of planning, documentation, governance and increasing overhead. The endless lists that characterise project management books, articles and manuals fuel this apprehension. There is the belief, too, that the so-called softer areas of organisation change and its political processes are simply not conducive to mechanistic input and output analysis or "engineered change". And in the more creative quarters, there is a fear that project management's organised approach to work, can only stifle any potential for innovation.

It is in the nature of our work as organisational consultants to focus on what makes projects succeed, and what prevent progress, and to apply techniques that bring maximum benefit and impact to a project in the immediate and the long term. We have written this book on the back of our experience as consultants, project managers and consultants to projects. We have written for those who are looking to be helped but not swamped.

The book is based on certain assumptions about you, the reader. We assume that you have an interest or responsibility for delivering a project that is about change. You have to engage the support of people over whom you have no direct control. Your project may be at the front end of change, for example the development of strategy and policy, or the design of new services. It could be focussed on the implementation of changes already agreed at the highest level, for example implementing a new service or new organisation. The project could be part of an MBA or to get a professional certification. Your project is not likely to be focussed on capital investment although capital issues may be a part of what you need to manage. We also assume that you will not have had much in the way of formal project management training.

Our aim is to help you extract from the general field of project management those elements that really fit your need. We concentrate on the relationship between change and project management given that so many projects are concerned either directly or indirectly with changing the ways in which people behave and perform. We also have a particular interest in the people aspects of project management because it is the area which produces so many problems in project work.

The characteristics of change projects throw up real dilemmas for project managers. Significant change causes turbulence. It tests commitment and resolve. It requires pace and momentum. Well-meaning project managers can become quickly frustrated by lack of clarity on objectives, on what approach to adopt, and on the failure of people to commit. We take the view that project managers can proactively manage these issues and that the skills to do so can become part of their key competencies.

Our chapters address key issues within project management and provide pointers on what to do. We base our work on research and our own experience. In particular we emphasise clear, up front thinking on the purpose of the project and its intended benefits, the detail of what needs to be delivered within the project and all the required activities. This is what you expect in a book on project management. But we explore more fully than most books, the skills of process thinking, contracting with clients and sponsors and how to factor in change management methods in a structured, conscious way. As good management practice feeds good project management, the reverse is also true. Most of these concepts will work for you beyond the project context and we expect you to derive broad benefit from our approach.

The structure of the book is important. We want to differentiate between those elements that we consider the Core parts of the discipline of project management irrespective of the size and complexity of the work, and those elements that come into play with the larger more demanding ventures.

There is a chapter on each of these themes, written to assist you in developing your own approach. Each chapter begins with a summary of how we hope it will help you. We draw upon theory but also make reference to case studies that come from our experience of working with clients. Each chapter finishes with some questions to help you think through your project and plan what to do next. Each chapter stands alone but cross references are made because, despite the sequential nature of project work, you will always find you have to manage more than one process at the same time.

As you read this book you may become aware of some management thinkers and consultants who over the years have had some profound impact on the ways in which we operate as project managers and change consultants. We would particularly like to single out Peter Block (for his work on developing partnerships with clients and how to contract successfully), William Bridges (for his work on change management), Meredith Belbin (for his work on team effectiveness), Edgar Schein on group processes, and Charles Kepner and Ben Tregoe for their work on group problem solving, decision making and planning.

We acknowledge with thanks their work and others and provide an additional reading list at the end for those of you who wish to pursue issues further.

Our contribution is meant to complement the formal and traditional project management approach enshrined by particular methodologies such as Prince 2. Moreover there are innumerable project management tools and techniques already covered by other books and training materials; for example the use of critical path analysis in planning. We do not seek to replicate these aspects.

We hope that you will find the material easy to follow and useful. We also hope that you might wish to provide us with your views and suggestions on how we could improve the work, and we invite you to do so.

Simon Standish
Change fx Ltd
simon.standish@change-fx.com

Pat Pegg Jones
White Eagle Ltd
PPeggJones@aol.com

London
April 2006

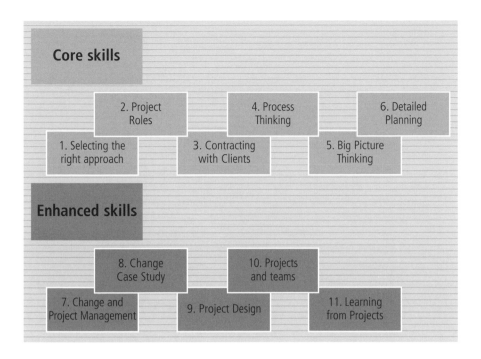

Core skills

2. Project Roles

4. Process Thinking

6. Detailed Planning

1. Selecting the right approach

3. Contracting with Clients

5. Big Picture Thinking

Enhanced skills

8. Change Case Study

10. Projects and teams

7. Change and Project Management

9. Project Design

11. Learning from Projects

Chapter One

The Challenge of Project Management

How will this chapter help you?

We want you to think about your project and your own skills in a different way. To help you do this, we set out some starting definitions and characteristics for projects, project management and change management. We describe a range of approaches you might take and then apply them. Finally, we ask you to assess your own project and your development needs. In this way you will be able to plan how you want to use the rest of the book.

What do we mean by project work?

There are certain characteristics that make project work special. Generally, projects entail work that is required within a specific time period with such work having a clear start and finish with clear assessable performance criteria. Ask any experienced project manager for a definition and they will say that it is the completion of work to time, cost and quality.

But these characteristics might apply to all work. Serving a customer or treating a patient could be seen as a project and might well benefit from some of the disciplines that we will be talking about later; but we will not be concentrating on this kind of work. Let us add some qualifying criteria.

We think of projects as having one or more of the following characteristics:

- **A significant piece of work with a client to be served**

- **A one off requirement that could not be delivered by the current organisational arrangements**

- **Work that is done by a team drawn from across groups that do not customarily combine**

- **Work whose scale and risk requires greater precision in the way that it is planned and managed**

- **Work that is aimed to secure change of one kind or another**

- **Work with an intensity of effort to meet tight deadlines**

There are also certain behavioural characteristics associated with project work. Projects have a clear focus on achieving delivery that requires behaviours that actively promote and drive the work forward. Therefore, success will be dependent upon clarity in terms of what needs to be done, swift decision making and a driving mentality about timescales. The project environment is a task focussed environment with relationships forming on the basis of intention and motivation around the task. This normally means being much more explicit about what is needed from individuals, with much more rapid feedback on performance, especially when things are not going to plan.

Another important behavioural characteristic is the ability of the project manager and team to recognise that their role exists within the limitations of terms of reference and time. A certain emotional detachment is required and an acceptance that some things within the project can be controlled and some things provoked by the project are out of scope and need to be left alone. The management of these work and emotional boundaries is an important characteristic of projects.

This leads to a final characteristic of projects, that being related to change. Most projects ultimately require change of people in terms of behaviour and performance; indeed it is hard to imagine a project that is not about change of this kind. New policies and strategies are intended in time to lead to new services and ways of doing things. New buildings and equipment will lead to changing roles, contributions and performance. This is why we take "people change" as a key characteristic of project work and why we integrate project and change management approaches.

So what is project management?

Project management is an umbrella term for a set of tools and techniques to support the planning and delivery of project work. These tools and techniques fall under three headings:

- **Planning** The thinking that is involved in achieving clarity on aims, objectives, method, activities and resources supported by precise tools for documenting and communicating plans (for example Gantt charts and critical path analysis). In addition, planning includes engagement and agreement with clients on the work to be done

- **Organising** Approaches to organising the management and delivery of the work including such notions as steering groups, project managers and project groups

- **Controlling** The processes and activities that ensure effective and efficient execution of work during the project's life; such things as general communication, evaluation, and performance management

And what about change management?

Project management tools and techniques are very good in planning and delivering a new living or working environment, for example new offices, production facilities and new computer programs. However, the approach on its own does not really address the psychology of change, the ways in which people react to changes and how that influences the rate at which a project can progress. The focus of change management is on enabling individuals and groups to understand and commit to different futures brought about by altered environments; for example helping with redefining working practices to operate in a newly designed production facility.

We divide change management tools and techniques into two broad categories:

- **Analysis** Techniques for assessing the individual and corporate psychology of change, people's preparedness and willingness for change and key areas of resistance. Tools for thinking about phases of change that might be orchestrated during the project to secure sustained new ways of doing things

- **Communication/engagement** This is the doing part of change management with tools and techniques for engaging people in the shaping and implementation of change (ranging from assessing the current, visioning the future, and moving from design to implementation)

Whilst project management owes its origin to structured engineering thinking, change management has its origins in behavioural science. We consider the integration of the two mentalities, tools and techniques to be key for the success of projects that ultimately hinge around new behaviours. From here on, when we talk about project management, we assume the effective integration of both approaches.

What is the range of project management approaches?
We view project management as a way of thinking, as well as a way of organising. It draws upon a range of tools and techniques, but the approach needs to be applied with flexibility.

A Core Approach or minimum requirement should be applied to any project. The more demanding projects will require a progressive application of tools and techniques pulled down from the full "menu" of project management. The diagram illustrates a progressive application of tools and techniques moving from the Core Approach towards a Full Application dependent upon an assessment of each project's scale and complexity. Assessing what a project needs in order to succeed is a fundamental skill for project managers and is considered in more detail later in the chapter.

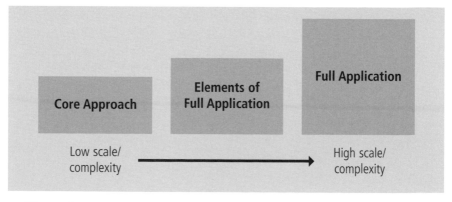

Diagram 1

Core Approach

The Core Approach treats project management much more as a set of thinking tools and disciplines with a very light weight touch on formal organisation and project bureaucracy.

All projects should have a clear:

- Context, terms of reference and objectives

- Method and process with timed/scheduled activities

- Identified client who will take decisions on change or sign off delivery

- A project lead who may carry the title manager or not

- Identified resources to undertake the work

In terms of personal skills you will need to be able to:

- Negotiate a realistic contract with clients

- Understand context for projects and be able to establish with clarity the objectives and benefits to be obtained from the project

- Describe the outputs or products required during the project

- Think in process terms about the approach and therefore to be able to identify the activities required and to schedule them

- Be clear about the role of project leader or manager

Full Application

Process/tools	• Business case
	• Scoping and terms of reference
	• Objective setting
	• Change management planning and interventions (the psychology of people change)
	• Method planning
	• Phasing analysis
	• Process and activity planning/scheduling
	• Gantt charts and critical path analysis
	• Risk assessments
	• Comprehensive budgeting
	• Third party negotiations
	• Performance management, evaluation and appraisal
Documentation	• Business case
	• Project Initiation Document
	• Change control documentation
	• Project Performance reporting (high and lower levels)
	• Budget schedules
	• Commercial contracts with third parties
	• Change management logs
	• Project close out and handover
Organisation	• Client
	• Project Sponsor
	• Steering Group
	• QA Group
	• Project Manager
	• Project Team
	• Project Office

Table 1

Full Application

At the other end of the spectrum we have a highly structured and formalised approach that applies more project management disciplines in order to maximise project impact in complex and risky environments. This "fuller" approach represents heavy investment in process, organisation and documentation as well as personal skills and organisational commitment. Table 1 sets out the features of the Full Application.

The movement to the more sophisticated and fuller application of project management requires additional management skills; those being the ability to:

- Understand the nature of change projects and be able to integrate processes of successful change management into the project

- Set up and manage teamworking for personnel for whom you are not the line manager

- Select the right organisational form for project to encompass sponsorship, management and technical doing

- Learn and improve within the project life

Enhanced Core Approach

In reality, many projects are set up and run with what we term an Enhanced Core Approach, drawing upon elements of the Full Application where appropriate. For example, many non capital projects might well have a dedicated project manager with a part time project team and be subject to many of the planning disciplines enshrined in the Project Initiation Document, but without a dedicated project office and full control and change management process or dedicated budgets.

The decision on the appropriate project management approach will reflect your assessment of the relative scale and complexity of your project. This assessment will say something about the skills you need to manage in this environment.

Before you undertake the assessment, we want to have a look at typical projects and their associated scale and risk factors.

What kind of project are you undertaking?

Project management gained early recognition within engineering disciplines, where the prevailing mentalities favoured a highly structured approach to planning and organising work associated with design and build remits. Over the years, its merits have led both private and public sector organisations to apply project management in conditions where the normal way of working would not deliver the results. In fact, project based working is likely to be the favoured line of attack where:

- Time for delivery is key

- Speedy, more creative solutions are required

- Wider participation and ownership of change is needed

- Customary relationships and organisation may stifle rather than encourage innovation and change

Projects are often used to provide developmental opportunities for up and coming members of staff or to offer a test bed for new ways of organising in the future.

As a current or aspiring project manager you may well be working on new:

- Policy or strategy

- Services or products

- Working or organisational arrangements

- Business processes or systems

- Facilities (new buildings, equipment or overhaul maintenance)

Your projects may well encompass a number of these elements. Let us take the relative scale and complexity issues.

Scale is easier to assess than complexity. An obvious indicator of scale is the range of resource assumed by the project during its life. Large capital intensive projects, like the construction of a hospital wing, will command much more resource than the development of new corporate policy. Another scale issue is the extent of impact on the organisation or system. A very focused change on a specific part of the production process is not of the same scale as the design and implementation of a complete process. So scale will be a function of:

- Resource required (people, materials)

- Impact and reach, be that financial (future income streams or costs), people (numbers affected), or political (other organisations and systems)

Complexity on the other hand is likely to be a function of:

- The number of clients, stakeholders and organisations involved and the degree to which there is likely to be divergence of view

- The nature of change required by the project and the degree of contention in terms of impact on jobs and behaviour

- The degree to which the project is in new undefined territory as opposed to using methods that are tried and tested.

- The degree to which your project is part of a broader more complicated system

- The number of activities being undertaken by different groups within different organisations

The assessment of scale and complexity can be used to help you determine the appropriate approach as indicated by the following grid.

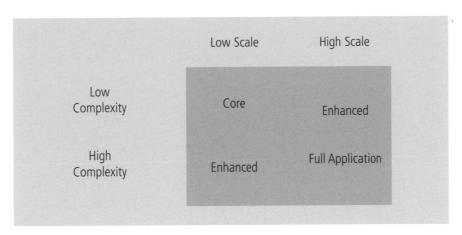

Diagram 2

Summary

Project work differs from regular on going work in a number of ways. The approach assumes disciplines and behaviours that are dedicated to delivering products within specified time periods. Traditional project management tools and techniques are very good at planning and delivering environmental change, but the behavioural issues require a different kind of thinking. Our approach is to integrate the tools and techniques of change management to form a broader approach that offers flexibility to meet the differing scale and complexity of projects. Core Approach, Enhanced Application and Full Application each demand different levels of organisational commitment and personal investment in terms of time and skills.

Now it is your turn!

Try the following questions:

1. **What kind of project do you have (policy, strategy, re-design of service, service improvement or what)? What kind of work does it assume?**

2. **How risky does it feel? How would you rate the scale and complexity of your project?**

3. **What kind of project management approach do you think you will have to take (core, enhanced, full)? Which tools, organisation, or documentation do you believe will be appropriate or necessary?**

4. **What key skills do you think that you need to work on in the first instance?**

Chapter Two

Project Roles

How will this chapter help you?

In the last chapter we set out a list of defining characteristics of project work. Included within the list is the reference to a "client" to be served and teamwork undertaken across normal organisational boundaries. The aim of this chapter is to help you think through important roles that need to be played in your project, and to help you consider what you need to negotiate as the project lead or manager.

Case study

For all the exhilaration of being associated with important change work, the role of the project manager can often be frustrating and down right risky. You may experience lonely moments when you are just not sure that you are on the right track. You may feel overworked and anxious about deadlines with a feeling of being powerless to do anything about it. You may feel exposed without much support and acknowledgement by others of the situation, and without a shared responsibility for doing something about it.

Just consider the following case study involving a discussion between Louise, a project manager, and Rachel, a close colleague.

Rachel   Louise, you look really tired – what's been happening?

Louise   Where do I start? The project is behind schedule and I can't get anyone to authorise additional resources. I go to the department heads and they pass me off. My sponsor hasn't been available for two weeks and I know that he would expect me to sort this but I can't. The Steering Group hasn't met for a month and they were barely quorate at the last meeting. I am getting fed up. On top of all this, my other work is beginning to suffer, and I never seem to have time for my family!

Rachel   Who knows that you are running behind schedule and are they concerned?

Louise   Well, I haven't issued a formal report yet but I am not sure who really would be concerned. It's been a while since the Chief Executive and the management team have made mention of this project so I don't know where this fits with their agenda.

Rachel   How much support have you been getting?

Louise   The Steering Group signed off on the project and many members of the Exec sit on the Steering Group. The project plan was pretty clear on the work and the timescales and I was given a budget for external support. But there was no real budget for internal staff time from the departments and that is where I am running into trouble. Staff members have been nominally assigned but I have no formal authority over them and it seems to be down to begging and stealing. What is more, when some staff do respond they do the bare minimum. There doesn't seem to be much that I can do.

Rachel   How important is this project then for them?

Louise   Well, for some it is their future but you would never guess!

Rachel   Who do you report to?

Louise   To Roger, the Head of Business Development. Nice guy. He has always spoken very positively about the future prospects for this service. But there is a rumour that he is going and of course some senior people may wish to review the prospects again for the project.

Rachel   So who do you think you need to talk to about this?

Louise   I think it must be Roger in the first instance but maybe the Chief Executive, if Roger is really going. I don't really know, maybe my Director.

This brief dialogue between Rachel and Louise touches on some crucial issues for project manager's role, authority and accountability. But Louise's issues also highlight the key contribution that others play within a project to give it direction, to sign off on propositions and to ensure that the work is resourced and supported. It seems a very confused state of affairs within this case.

We want to examine four roles in particular. Two of the roles reflect the customer perspective and the other two, a supplier perspective.

Customer Perspective

Having an identified customer or client is vital to the sanity of the project manager, who as the one who will deliver the project, is in the role of the supplier. Clarity on these roles is fundamental to the success of the project. Generally it is the client (and we will use this term from now on) who will be called upon to determine:

- What is required (in terms of the end product)
- Conditions for satisfactory delivery (quality and timing issues)
- Budget for delivery

Early on the **supplier** needs to negotiate and reach agreement with the client about the requirements. This is an initial step in the supplier's prime task of taking the requirements and working up proposals for achieving them.

The notion of clients for projects sits easily with organisations that are in the business of providing products and services to external clients or customers. It is part of a service organisation's culture that clients are to be served. In other organisations, the concept of a client has less common currency. This is especially true for the large corporate or public sector head offices where staff may be somewhat removed from end users and customers, and where the idea of an internal clients seems to suggest an unwelcome hierarchy of power and interest.

We believe that the notion and dynamics of a client relationship is an important focal point in project work. Our definition of a client is someone who fulfils one or more of the following.

In project work, the **client** :

- **Fundamentally wants the project undertaken**
- **Is in a position to determine what the project needs to deliver**
- **May fund the project**
- **Will own the product of the project and often will be responsible in some way for its longer term use**
- **Has the authority to sign off on delivery or agree variations to project plan**

Stakeholders

Let us consider another role, one that is often confused with the client role, and that is the stakeholder.

The term stakeholder embraces those individuals, groups and organisations who consider that they have a legitimate stake or interest in the outcome of the project. Indeed, some will have profound impact on the success or failure of the venture. The **stakeholders** might:

- **Consume or use products and services affected by the project**
- **Regulate the way in which products or services are delivered (for example health and safety regulators).**
- **Be impacted by the outcomes of the project (for example staff whose role or activities change as a result of a project)**

For any given project, there may be a multitude of different stakeholders with differing requirements, preoccupations and concerns. They will also differ in terms of their relative impact on the success of the project.

Let's take an example.

A joint initiative of a local authority and a health organisation might be the development and delivery of a health promotion package for younger mothers to assist in their care of very young children.

The stakeholders for such a project are likely to be:

- Current young mothers or prospective mothers
- Health visitors
- Community workers
- Voluntary organisations and their members
- Public health specialists
- Community paediatricians

The stakeholders might be categorised in the following way:

- Net beneficiaries of the health promotion package (younger mothers and their children)
- Regulators (Public Health Specialists)
- Bankers (the Finance Directors)
- Ultimate deliverers of the package (health visitors, paediatricians, the voluntary organisations)

Their requirements will be different and may not be compatible:

- Younger mothers must have something that is useful and practical
- Public Health specialists want to ensure that the product is based on evidence and best practice and makes a difference to overall health and well being
- The Finance Director wants to ensure that the product is affordable
- Healthcare professionals want to ensure that the product can be delivered with the current skills or that their skills will be enhanced appropriately

The tensions underlying these different perspectives and requirements can be considerable and need to be managed. Moreover, a position on relative priorities has to be formulated by someone.

The task of managing and prioritising Stakeholder requirements is the Client's responsibility.

The solution to the pressures of stakeholder interests in the public sector is often to set up a **Steering Group** where a broad range of interests can be represented. This may work fine if the group is not too large, or if there is a strong chair who is prepared to arbitrate on competing requirements and claims (and de facto play the client role). It can be the stuff of nightmares for the supplier however, if arbitration is not managed. When that happens, the supplier, internal or external, is left with the task of integrating the requirements. This shows one reason why understanding the distinction between the Client's responsibilities and the Project Manager's responsibilities is so important.

In the case of the health promotion product, the Steering Group might comprise senior directors who have responsibility for implementing and managing aspects of the health promotion programme, joined by an independent party acting on behalf of the users. It is this group who will have responsibility for signing off the recommended programme and for ensuring funding for its development.

Supplier Roles

We turn next to roles that are concerned with the delivery of the project, those being the **project sponsor** and **project manager**. Not all projects require these two roles, but in order to illuminate the roles and the functions we will cover both.

A **Project Sponsor** is normally a senior individual in an organisation whose role is to:

- **Give senior leadership to the delivery of the project**

- **Champion the cause of the project and by doing so give it priority within the organisation**

- **Ensure that resources are unlocked**

- **Provide mentorship and guidance to more inexperienced project managers**

The best analogy for understanding the Sponsor role is to look at the Chair and Chief Executive roles in organisations where these roles are split. The Chair manages many of the external interfaces and politics and the Chief Executive becomes the chief operating officer responsible for the day to day delivery. The Project Sponsor is similar to the Chair in that they provide a semi-detached senior check and balance for more detailed work being undertaken by the Project Manager who acts as CEO to the project.

Not all projects require a Sponsor but it is a very useful role in conditions where:

- The project manager may not have the perceived authority and clout to resolve difficult conflicts involving more senior players in the organisation or in other organisations

- Complex and larger scale projects where the risks are high and where senior level directors need to be in command of what is happening

• There is a relatively inexperienced Project Manager

A senior level group, such as a senior management team, might provide sponsorship collectively. This body is also sometimes called a Steering Group, but has a very different function to a Steering Group comprised of stakeholders. However, given the conditions above, access to one named and skilled sponsor may be a more practical and effective approach.

Going back to the Health Promotion case, the sponsor of the project might well be the Public Health or Service Development Director given that much of the resource going into the project may come from their areas. They will also be senior enough to ensure access for the project manager to other directorates and organisations to acquire resources to achieve the programme development.

The reason for differentiating between a Client and a Sponsor is to separate the supply of a solution (the project) from the demand for it (coming from the customer or client). This separation is necessary in situations where decisions are required on the trade offs around time or quality of solution or the cost of providing it. It is the Clients who must determine what they will accept in the end. If the client and sponsorship roles are combined then the sharpness of the client requirement can be compromised by the intricacies of the supplier dilemma. It is important to note, that in many projects, this distinction is lost when a sponsor is appointed who straddles both roles.

The Project Manager

In its purest manifestation, the Project Manager will be responsible both for the way in which the project is established and run (the process), and for the specific results achieved (the content). We can break that down in the following way:

Process

• **Developing and getting agreement to the project scope, objectives and approach**

• **Developing and getting agreement for the project plan and resourcing**

• **Setting up processes of quality assurance and performance management**

• **Marshalling resources (staff and others) and making good use of them**

• **Reporting to the sponsor and clients on progress and making changes in plans are required**

Content

- **Meeting the technical and financial targets for deliverables within the plan**

- **Quality assuring the delivery to make sure that it fits the client requirement**

- **Making appropriate changes when problems or alterations in external circumstances occur**

In Chapter One we introduced the notion of assessing a project's scale and complexity to determine the overall project approach. This assessment will also govern the approach taken to time commitment and role of the Project Manager.

The Project Management role in practice may vary in the degree to which the project manager has:

- Direct control on staff resource and is able to select whom they wanted

- Responsibility for the appraisal and development of staff

- A budget for the project and that this budget covers all or some of the costs

- Authority to enter into third party contracts

- Authority to decide policy and operational issues without reference to the sponsors or clients

The Project Manager could be full or part time. For the smaller, less risky and complex projects, project managers may be part time, operating with limited and rather loose arrangements with other departments or organisations for access to staff. Indeed, some Project Managers will not even have the title "manager" being seen rather as "co-ordinators" of work.

For larger more complex projects, the Project Manager is likely to be full time, supported by a project office with the full budget responsibilities and a clear schedule of authorities.

Authority and the Project Manager

The issue of authority arises within the project environment because it is in the very nature of project work that it cuts across normal lines of management. The title Project Manager implies responsibility, accountability and authority to see a project through to completion. Yet one of the most frequent complaints expressed is the feeling of lack of authority. In fact, it is important to note here that helplessness is probably one of the feelings most often complained of by Project Managers in organisations.

In organisations where projects are a normal way of getting work done, there may be less contention around the role and authority of the Project Manager. This is particularly seen for example in construction and consulting settings, or any service organisation that is structured to serve external clients on a project by project basis. But for many organisations the notion that a Project Manager should be able to command resource on a limited time basis from a range of internal departments, flies in the face of customary ownership and control of resource. So the question of authority is a rapidly escalating issue and one that is personally and politically charged.

The Project Manager has four sources of authority. The first is derived from the credibility and standing of the project within the organisation. This might be determined by examining the level of buy in and support from the Board or the Executive Team for the project. One indication of this will be in the extent to which senior members communicate the project to their teams and, too, how much prominence is given to the project.

The second source of authority is derived from the political power of those who are Clients or Sponsors of the project. This is really trading on the basis of the power and authority of those who have commissioned the work, where the Project Manager is seen as the Director's "representative on earth".

The third source of authority will be the formal delegation of decision making and responsibility to the Project Manager as part of a project set-up process.

Each of these sources of authority can be subject to negotiation at the beginning of the project. For example, in meeting with the client/sponsor, you may wish to negotiate:

- Communication by senior Directors on the importance of the project and their expectations of support from the organisation

- The composition of the Steering Group to ensure that important resource providers have a stake in the outcome

- When the Steering Group meets in order to ensure swift appraisal of issues and problem solving

- How discussion and agreed action gets disseminated through the organisation to ease follow up by the project manager

- Frequency of meetings between the project manager and client/sponsor to aid informal decision making and problem solving

- The resourcing budget and definition of responsibilities for the project together with how this is communicated

Negotiation is dealt with in the next chapter (Client Contracting).

The fourth source of authority is derived from the personal skills and network of the

Project Manager; for example:

- Being skilled in project management with a visible track record and commitment to achievement of results

- Being on top of the project and in command of what is going on

- Being networked to the clients and stakeholders and on top of general developments surrounding the project

- Having an up front presence with stakeholders and being able to communicate with clarity on the project

- Having a clear view of what is needed from others but what you offer as a project manager to them

Understanding and valuing this personal source enhances the Project Manager's influence both inside and outside the organisation.

Summary on key project roles

We have described two customer or client oriented roles – Client and Stakeholders – and two roles associated with the delivery of the project – Sponsor and Project Manager. It is vital to be clear on each of these roles in a project and who is playing it. Without an overall Client, the Stakeholder requirement may become unmanageable. Without a senior Sponsor, the Project Manager may be unable to gain resource and resolve cross boundary issues. And if the roles of Client and Sponsor are combined, then the Project Manager will have to be clear on which role is being played in every interaction and meeting.

Now it's your turn!

Think of your project

1. **Who would you see as your client? Why? What is this based on? To what extent does that person – your client – recognise their part and their responsibilities?**

2. **Who are the key stakeholders (individuals and groups)? What are their points of interest and requirements? How difficult will it be to harmonise these requirements?**

3. **Is there a need for a sponsor for your project? For what reasons? Who might that be?**

4. How do you see your role as the Project Manager? What level of authority and responsibility do you need? Who will you negotiate with on this? What kind of time commitment do you think you will need to fulfil the role?

5. What excites and scares you about this project? What do you think you will have to negotiate?

Chapter Three

Contracting with Clients

How will this chapter help you?

Contracting will be a key feature of your life as a project manager. It dominates the preparation and set up phases of your project, and it will recur throughout delivery and as you bring your project to a close. Contracting is a broad term, covering information gathering, the exchange of expectations, the addressing of concerns and negotiating to an agreement. You will contract for what you do and how you do it, but you will also be seeking to influence and build relationships through the process. The relationships you establish will be very important in handling and resolving problems as they arise. If you are skilled, you will end up with a realistic and achievable project proposition with enthusiastic and supportive clients and sponsors who feel themselves to be partners in the enterprise. The process can be problematic, especially if you are an internally appointed project manager having to negotiate with people senior to yourself in the organisation. You have more influence than you think, however, and it is our aim in this chapter to help you realise it.

We will do this by saying more about the focus of contracting during a project, and then describe the mentality and the skill set required. We then offer examples of application of the process in the early stages of a project. Finally, we ask you to consider your own project and to think about what you need to do to contract for success.

The Focus of Contracting during a Project

The previous chapter on Project Roles examined the responsibilities of clients, sponsors and project managers.

- **Clients** have the responsibility to be clear on what they require, taking into consideration their own needs and the needs and wants of other key external stakeholders. They are custodians of the resulting specification and it is the Client who agrees any changes.

- **Sponsors** have the responsibility to ensure senior management championing of the project, that the plans are clear and that resources are made available. They also have senior level responsibility for assuring the method to be used and delivery of the project.

- **Project Managers** have the responsibility of developing robust and realistic plans for delivery and for managing allocated resources to achieve the specification.

We recognise it can happen that one person may play the client and sponsor role.

An effective contracting process enables specific agreement and understanding on project issues whilst at the same time establishing a relationship that is conducive to the sharing of underlying and more difficult points. In the table below we show the topics and themes that arise explicitly in early discussion, and those attitudes and beliefs we call "below the surface". These might take more time to surface on their own. We believe they need to be put on the table by the Project Managers as part of the contracting discussion. Agreement on project issues tends to be more up front, rational, explicit, and documented. Underlying attitudes and beliefs are often unstated but observable. They also have enormous potential to impact adversely on the process and outcome of the project if not addressed constructively. An essential part of our contracting proposition is that underlying beliefs and attitudes should be tested explicitly and be the subject, or the basis, of agreement.

Explicit discussion	• Project Terms of reference
	• Objectives – long and short term
	• Time / quality / cost criteria
	• Approach to project
	• Resources and budgets
	• Reporting arrangements
	• Approvals/authorities
Beneath the surface attitudes and beliefs	
	• Perception of risks
	• Levels of motivation and commitment
	• Concerns, doubts, reservations
	• Perceived levels of support
	• Trust and confidentiality issues
	• Politics and relationships

Table 2

In terms of contracting there will be a continuing dialogue between the Project Manager and the Client/Sponsor through the following key phases of the project:

- Pre-Project start-up (through exploration and agreement)

- Project delivery

- Project closure and handover

Table 3 summarises the purpose of each of these stages from a contracting perspective.

Contracting as a process

Contracting is an umbrella term covering information gathering, the exploration of wants, expectations and concerns, through to bargaining and negotiating. The product of the process is an agreement with a joint understanding on what has been agreed and what are important issues for the work (we stress the distinction between reaching joint understanding and assuming common understanding!). The agreement and understandings may be enshrined within a formal contract; this is certainly the case

Phase	Pre-Project Start Up		Post Start Up	
	Exploration	**Agreement**	**Delivery**	**Close out**
Aim	• Understanding the context for the project • Establishing a working relationship based upon the notion of partnership	• Agreement on the scope, deliverables and the resourcing • Agreement on organisation, governance and communications • Achieving confidence in project and arrangements • Achieving confidence and trust between the client and project manager	• Agreement on changes that need to be made • Getting feedback and recognition for work • Ensuring continued support for the project • Keeping on track as project achieves milestones or encounters difficulties	• Agreeing handover and legacy issues • Ensuring satisfaction with result • Getting feedback and recognition
Communication Focus	• Exploration and understanding • Questions to understand • Sharing of information • Why and what if	• Negotiation and agreement on the project content and process • Proposing • Testing • What if.....then	• Problem solving • Negotiating changes • Review questions • Why questions • What now needs to be done	• Learning • Negotiation on handover • What is left to be done • What, who and when questions

Table 3

if you are an external supplier. For the internal project manager, whether or not agreements are formalised tends to reflect the culture of the organisation. Having an explicit contract has particular value for a complex project being undertaken in a chaotic environment.

Contracting is a mind set as well as a skill set. Let us take the mindset first.

Successful contracting assumes a mentality of:

- **Partnership working and mutual responsibility.** There may be a presumption that the client knows best and that the client should take the lead. Successful project managers do not assume this. They strive for a partnership with clients not based on hierarchy or seniority but on shared responsibility for the outcome of the project.

- **An obsession with clarity on product, process and role.** The contracting mentality is one of making explicit what is really needed to deliver the project. This works at the macro level for project plans and reviews as well as at the micro level for each meeting and engagement that is undertaken.

• **Putting into words what you want and need.** Project work differs markedly from ordinary line work. The supplier and client relationship requires that players communicate freely on what is needed to achieve a successful solution, as well as to share threats or consequences as they are seen. This means speaking one's mind, even if it contradicts the more powerful client or sponsor. Projects often fail due to unrealistic expectations about delivery founded on unrealistic estimates of capacity and capability. The project manager needs to assert how they see the situation and to inspire an open dialogue about realities.

• **The ability to acknowledge contribution but also to confront poor performance.** While contracting assumes agreement on roles, responsibility and action, project managers are always seeking further engagement and contribution to take the project forward. A key mentality is the recognition of behaviour and performance that adds to project progress. Follow through by the project manager is needed to recognise and reward positive contributions. There is also a requirement to confront non compliance or poor performance within the context of negotiated and agreed contracts with individuals or teams.

• **The ability to say no.** This is a most difficult and uncomfortable mentality for project managers. It calls for a clear view by the manager on boundaries, what is in and what is out. Sometimes what belongs within the project boundary is clear, and sometimes it requires evaluation or negotiation. There will be times, however, when an idea, suggestion, or change can not be accommodated without serious consequences. This is the time when the Project Manager must protect the integrity and viability of the plan.

Table 4 illustrates how you might see these mentalities played out in meetings.

	Behaviours that demonstrate contracting mentality	Behaviours that don't indicate contracting mentality
Partnership	• Balance of air time • Taking turns in initiating and proposing • "If I... then you" • Listening and supporting • Critical but appreciative • Use of "we"	• Dominance by one • Cutting across speech • Imposition of ideas and action • Absence of challenge • Monologues • Use of "I" and "you"
Clarity on product, process and role	• Use of clarification questions or statements • Use of summary at key points • Challenging for clarity • Confirmation on action • Agreement on use of time and agenda for meetings • Use of "I" and "you" to confirm actions	• Open ended discussions • Moving on to next agenda without closure • Imprecise discussion on who • Issues raised but not grounded
Communication of needs and wants	• Assertive interpretations of impact of decisions • Calls to reflect • Perseverance with detailed implications • Use of "I/we need and want...." • Use of questions to probe thinking	• Silence but look of concern • Acceptance of requirements without clarification or challenge • Never moving into the detail
Recognition of contribution	• Comment on contribution and its impact • Comment on performance shortfalls • Communication of pleasure and disappointment	• Avoidance of issues • Making good others' poor performance • Comment on performance to other parties but not direct
Saying no	• Saying "no" • Reflection on requirements and then reference to prior agreements • Challenging assumptions	• Silent acquiescence • Reflection or repetition of other party's requirements without comment

Table 4

Critical skills

There are also some critical thinking and communication skills. They include the ability to:

- **Empathise.** The ability to assess a situation and to understand the issues from a number of viewpoints.

- **Use a range of questions.** The ability to ask really good questions to understand others' thinking and to encourage others to elaborate on what might be very difficult issues. This is particularly important when it comes to probing resistant behaviour.

- **Listen and observe attentively.** The ability to listen effectively for what is said, but at the same time read non verbal communication to suggest other sentiments.

- **Present thought and ideas clearly and with influence.** The ability to communicate ideas and propositions clearly and assertively and being able to establish relevance for the project and the needs of clients or stakeholders. It includes using a range of presentational techniques to attract attention and response.

- **Frame musts and wants.** The ability to distinguish between those things that are really critical from those that are desirable.

- **Negotiate.** The ability to assess the room for give and take and to understand and communicate the implications when a trade is made.

- **Summarise and close.** The ability to re-state what has been discussed and agreed to ensure that there is genuine understanding and accord.

Contracting in the pre-start up phase
Exploration and Agreement

For some people, Contracting is something that takes place at a second, third or fourth meeting with the client, after preliminary sessions and when enough information exists to start negotiating details to construct a plan. Our stance is that Contracting starts at the beginning when project thinking may be embryonic and the client/project manager relationship hardly formed. We want to focus particularly on the pre-project start up phase (Exploration and Negotiation) since this establishes the foundation for a successful project.

The Exploration Stage

There are a number of good practices to adopt from the beginning:

- **Operate as a partner from the start.** It is important that as a Project Manager you structure meetings with the client from the very start. This will demonstrate in very practical terms a partnered approach to managing the early discussions.

- **Negotiate how you will work together with the client from the outset.** Even experienced people tend to go into meetings with a main aim of seeking the wants and information from their client. Your wants as project manager are as fundamental as those of the client.

- **Prepare your questions and contributions in advance.** Think through what you want to achieve in the early meetings and prepare what you will ask for with as much care as you prepare what you wish to get across.

Both parties should regard the early meetings as the time to clarify the context for the project and what it might entail. It is also an opportunity for the parties to begin to form strong relationships to underpin the project. From the project manager's perspective it is important to understand:

- Why the project is needed

- The degree of urgency

- Who are the stakeholders

- How complex is the project

- How big is it

- The expectations and the nature of the client

Table 5 sets out some key questions that project managers might want to ask clients in order to form judgements in each area.

Judgement area	Key Questions
Why this project?	• What is the problem or opportunity? • Why must the problem or opportunity be grasped? • How important is this to the organisation and why? • What benefits will flow and to whom?
Why now?	• What if no action is taken for the next year? • Who feels the pain of the problem now? • What are they saying about urgency?
Who are the interested parties?	• Who are the interested parties externally and internally? • What is their level of interest? • How might they like to be involved? • Who are the key players in terms of making this happen or with the ability to obstruct?
How complicated will it be?	• How clear is the problem, the causes, the options or the solution? • How compatible are the stakeholder interests?

	• Who might be affected and what might their reaction be?
	• Has this issue been looked at before?
	• If it has, what progress was made – why did it not get further?
	• Has this issue been grasped by other organisations and how successful have they been?
How big is this project?	• How much of the organisation is impacted or could be impacted by the project?
	• What is the potential scope of the project in terms of services and activities?
	• What are some of the obvious issues that must be addressed by the project?
	• How many organisations and people need to be actively involved?
What kind of client do I have?	• Did you initiate this project, if not who did?
	• Why is this project important to you?
	• What different would success or failure of this project make to you?
	• What role do you want to play?
	• How much time would you give this project?
	• What worries you about this?
	• What experience do you have of working these issues before?
	• What are you looking for from me as a project manager?
	• What experience do you have of working as a client or sponsor to a project?
	• Who are you accountable to? What are their concerns and pre-occupations?

Table 5

Doubts, Concerns, Resistance

You can see that some of the questions are objective enquiries about the project. However, talking to people about things that concern them usually means moving to more personal terrain. This means touching on issues of perceived risk and commitment, both of which may have profound impact on the successful management and delivery of the project.

For the Client, ownership of a project can sometimes mean:

• Loss of face or status if a project does not deliver its promised benefits

- Loss of control over how the project will be run

- Uncontrollable demands on their time

- Having to negotiate or beg others for resources

- Having to defend unconventional activity

- Loss of the comfort of straightforward line management command

Client concerns may manifest themselves in doubts, persistent questioning, and a general reluctance to move forward. These reactions or behaviours are not bad things in themselves, but they are signs of something that needs to be addressed. Being on the receiving end of resistance can feel uncomfortable, but you should not take it personally.

It is vital that you deal with concerns, reservations, and resistance constructively. It seems many people do not take a direct approach in expressing their concerns or may find it difficult to do so. Therefore, an important skill for the Project Manager is to enable the discussion of concerns and uncomfortable issues by:

- **Asking directly for concerns and reservations.** You should be prepared to model the open behaviour you want by sharing your own concerns.

- **Being receptive when the client tells you their doubts or concerns.** The news may be uncomfortable for you (their last project experience may have been a disaster, or you were their 4th choice for Project Manager, or they will be moving to another facility before the project is over); but their concerns are part of the context of the project, part of the collaborative relationship, and input to your working together as partners.

- **Going into a conversation about the concern.** You don't have to fix the situation or even give advice; in fact, we would encourage you not to give advice at this stage, but rather take the client's side by listening and by being understanding, compassionate and non judgemental.

Achieving a complete picture of the needs and desires of the client is very important for the Project Manager. If this does not happen early on, there is a danger that unexpected concerns or wants will emerge after start up, forming the basis for complications or variations to the original project specification. Understanding the client's range of need, the level of priority attached to each need and the underlying reasons helps the project manager prepare for the negotiation of resources and timescales and to explore other options.

The client will talk about their needs in relation to the output of the project, but they are certain to have concerns relating to their role and the extent of their involvement. Although we have stated that the client is responsible for clarity on the overall requirements for the project, many will take a particular interest in the way in which the project is conducted and will want to become involved in operational delivery. This may reflect their own experience and skills, or reflect underling issues of lack of trust and confidence in the project arrangements. The project manager may view such involvement as inappropriate and personally undermining. The best time to have a discussion on issues of style and interpretation of role is before the project starts rather than in the heat of the project moment.

The Negotiation Stage

You will know that you have moved from exploration to negotiation as you begin to propose elements that will form the basis of a contract or the detail of the project plan. Your overall objective at this stage should be to secure agreement on:

- What the project needs to achieve and deliver (and what is out of scope)

- The overall timescales for delivery

- The costs of delivery as evidenced by the process plan and resources required

- Your role as project manager and the role of the client

- How you will work together

The first three elements will be shaped by your earlier judgements in the exploratory phase combined with an assessment of the work and resources required. Later chapters in this book will help you with moving from the 'Big Picture' project overview to the more detailed project thinking.

How you will work with the client is a critical area for discussion and explicit agreement but is often overlooked. We encourage you to discuss and agree your formal and informal working arrangements; for example:

- How often you will see each other

- How much time you will commit to spending in meetings

- What kind of information you will share via other means

- What kind of response time is expected when things are really important

- How issues would be designated as being important and urgent

- How certain issues will be dealt with confidentiality

- In what ways will your client promote and champion the cause of the project with others

- What might require formal approval and how will it be secured

We spoke earlier in the chapter about "beneath the surface" issues of trust, confidence and commitment, all of which are key foundations for effective partnership working and the realisation of the project. These are intangible, ethereal qualities, so whilst it is not possible to contract for trust, for example, explicitly, it is possible to agree rules of engagement and operation that manifest them and that build the relationship.

We said that an important contracting mentality is the ability to say no. People often get nervous about this, as they do not wish to be seen as unhelpful or negative. For the internally appointed Project Manager working to a senior in the organisation, the prospect of saying no can be particularly daunting. However, project work will always require an authentic and assertive approach by the Project Manager. Framing the negative response authentically can be more than a straightforward rejection. Here are some alternatives to the categorical "no" that express a project manager's judgement, or that draw the client to make the final call:

- I don't know how to do that.

- I don't know how to do that within the constraints we have now.

- I can't do that by the time we need it. Can you help me adjust some priorities?

- I don't know how we can meet that date. What would happen if we were a week late?

- I don't know how to stay within schedule and budget if we change the requirements at this late date.

- We could do that. It would require more resources, and it would take longer, but we could do it.

- It's unlikely we could get it done. It's possible, but I'd estimate that the probability is less than 10%.

Many areas of project management require courage. In contracting, saying no is an area where the need for courage may well be the most obvious.

Summary

Contracting is a key process for project managers. It is a broad term covering information gathering, the exchange of expectations, the addressing of concerns and negotiating to an agreement. The process starts early in the life of a project as the project manager and the client meet to explore what may be involved. Contracting will focus on an agreement about content of the project as well as its process. A more subtle part of the contracting process is about developing a strong relationship between the project manager and the client that will underpin leadership and management of the venture through its life. Contracting is a mindset as well as a skill set, with a particular emphasis on seeing a partnership between the project manager and client. The pre start up phase of contracting is key to establishing a sound foundation for the project.

Case study

We illustrate below some of the key points of contracting in the pre start up exploration and negotiation stage. The dialogue is between Robyn, the Project Manager and Alex who is the client. The project in question focuses on the reduction of teenage pregnancy locally. We show the dialogue and in the margin refer to some of the key contracting points.

Robyn, Project Manager	Thank you for making the time to discuss this project with me, Alex. We haven't worked together before. I'm looking forward to it. I believe there is broad recognition of the importance of this project for young people in our area. I'd like to understand the context better, and to get a view of how you see the project. That's my hope for this meeting – that and to spend some time on how you and I will work together as the project progresses. How about you, what do you want to cover today?	Contracting for the meeting Setting expectations Looking at context but also relationships
Alex, Client	Yes, Robyn, this is "my" project – I've worked for several years to get this set up. I'm sure you know that the statistics for teenage pregnancy locally show it is a real problem. If we can reduce the numbers of unwanted pregnancies, we can make a difference to the prospects for young girls and avoid expensive dependency on local services over the coming years.	Looking at why the project is important Hinting at outcomes
Robyn	So the long term goal is to reduce teenage pregnancy. How do you see the project making impact on this?	Summary of long term goal or purpose of project Question to understand scope and content of project
Alex	We need to be clearer about the factors leading to current levels and sharpen our thinking on what will make the difference in future. I think we can anticipate a range of measures such as education of youngsters, different and more accessible contraception services, and assessment of the agencies that support termination if that is seen to be the right thing to do.	Scope and scale of project

Robyn	Let me get this clear then. The overall aim is to reduce unwanted teenage pregnancy. The project I'll be managing is an early step in that direction by identifying the causes of the current levels leading to recommendations on changes for services and spend. I presume those recommendations will be the key product of the project. Then what?	Summary of long term goal Summary of short term delivery or products Question to clarify scope
Alex	Well that is as far as I am thinking at the moment. This phase will take 6 months. And yes, I expect that recommendations will be an output of this project. There is a wide range of players and organisations. Once we create a strategy, it will be very important that it is based on good analysis and can be defended in public. We'll need the effective involvement of the key players.	Confirmation of scope and key product Additional criteria for success
Robyn	What is your idea about effective involvement? I can imagine who the key players might be, but who specifically do you have in mind?	Assessment of stakeholders Estimation of complexity of project
Alex	Social Services and we in the Primary Care Organisation are very committed. Lowering teenage pregnancy is part of the Public Service Agreement targets. The Local Strategic Partnership has communicated this issue as a priority for the year. The fly in the ointment is that some of the service providers are anxious about where this work might lead, that it may have consequences for their level of funding next year. It's been a tough budget for all of us.	Stakeholder commitment Caution and risk Contention leads to more complex process
Robyn	OK, I see that the Public Service Agreement targets and the fact that teenage pregnancy is a priority gives authority, even an urgency to the project. I know too, from past experience, that potential impact on other groups' operating budgets can generate mistrust and lack of cooperation. What else do you think is relevant at this stage?	Continued probing to understand scope and complexity issues Open question to probe relevant context
Alex	I'm going to be involved in a parallel assignment that may entail my being at another site approximately one week each month until Christmas. I've said this phase could take 6 months, but I'm hoping the key research can be achieved a bit faster than that.	Setting expectation on client role and access Setting expectation about timescales for delivery
Robyn	Well – that's not good news for me, but I'm glad to learn about your other work sooner rather than later. It will have implications for how we decide to work together.	

Alex	We need to take sufficient time, because the recommendation we come up with must be based on sound data. There are some key people we want to build into the project, who can help in the next stage of it. There are also some people who will actively block us if their views are not at least reflected in the final conclusions, and we need to include them too.	Building additional process into the project
Robyn	An early task for us will be for you to brief me on who those key people are, and what I need to know about them. Let's talk a bit about how the project will be run. What you want from me as Project Manager?	Developing the notion of partnership Probing to understand expectation of role
Alex	Since I most likely will be away more than I thought during the life of the project, I want to make sure our meetings are efficient.	Expectation of working process
Robyn	I like to think that I have a reasonable amount of experience in managing development projects but this area is pretty contentious and I don't have a good feel for all the complexities at this point. I'll need to be able to represent the project to people in several different organisations. So I would like to have regular sessions with you in the early stages to make sure that I am really covering the angles and reading the externals right. Could we agree to that?	Statement of wants and needs from Project Manager Negotiating on access to client
Alex	Yes of course and I will need some pretty rigorous reporting on this in order to keep our partners on board. Also Robyn, I need to know about problems early if I am going to manage the surround to this project	Assertion of needs from client
Robyn	I agree to that! There does not appear to be a budget for staff time on this. If I can specify who I need and how much of their time, will you sign off on it and then back up my requests to the other organisations?	Negotiating for budget and for specific client actions
Alex	Well yes within reason. Everyone is so pressed for time. There is always push back on such requests. You'll have better chance of success on that if you provide me with a good case for everything you ask for. I'll need that data.	Demonstration of partnership " If you…. then I"
Robyn	I'd also like to discuss a concern I have. I'm genuinely worried about how this work is fitting in with my regular duties in the directorate. I understand that you have agreed my time allocation on the project with my line Director. But he is pushing me very hard on two other pieces of work.	Putting concerns on the table
Alex	I did agree your project role with your boss Keith although I am not sure that we agreed 2 days per week. I will need to check this again but you will need to keep us both on board in terms of your loading.	Setting expectation about communication

Robyn	There may be times when I will need to get you both in the room! On the matter of the budget then, I will report against a sum of £25,000 but this will be enhanced to cover staff time and consumables.	Negotiation on access and budget
Alex	I don't know that there is any more in the bank for this but if you give me a schedule of who you need and how much of their time, then I will begin the campaign.	Asserting the partnership
Robyn	Alex, it's going to be very helpful if you could promote this project and my role in it through the organisation with some kind of communication to the other organisations. This will at least help establish the work and your commitment behind it. When I have got a more detailed project plan with resource assumptions for the next 3 months, could I come and present this to the management team? That should help cement things a little.	Asking for action to legitimise project and PM role externally Asking for access to other key decision makers
Alex	If you can draft something up for me, I can at least get the ball rolling.	
Robyn	I want to say that this has been a useful start to this project. You've made the background and the specific objectives of this project clearer for me – and that will help me in formulating the project plan. It will also help me in my discussions with other people about the project. I can't say that your extra assignment and the absence was good news, but I think it will be helpful in that it forces us to plan more precisely how we'll work together with the constraints we have.	Acknowledge client's contribution to the meeting

Now it is your turn

Think about your project

1. **Who is your client?**

2. **What do you need to find out about the project?**

3. **What do you need to know about your client?**

4. **What do you want your client to know about your strengths and experience?**

5. **What are the factors you feel even at this stage will be important for the success of the project?**

6. **At this stage what do you feel will be the tricky issues to negotiate?**

7. **How will you secure a close working relationship with your client?**

Chapter Four

Process Thinking

The foundation for successful Project Management

How will this chapter help you?

A recipe for cake making assumes a set of ingredients, kitchen technology and of course culinary skill. The recipe includes a process for working the ingredients into the prized product. In projects, having the right people, material and technology will be vital, but insufficient without an effective plan of attack based upon considered "process thinking". Indeed, in the early stages of a project, it is the plan that will initially inspire confidence for clients, sponsors and team members. Process thinking is a skill in its own right and demands a certain mentality. This chapter aims to help you understand what it entails so you can use the perspective early in consideration of your project. We start with some definitions of process, give examples and then, as usual, ask you to reflect on your project.

Introducing process thinking

Let's start with the analogy of the computer. At the heart of a computer is its operating system, its way of storing and manipulating data and images. On top of this, there are specific business applications (for example word processing and spreadsheets). These specific applications enable you to produce content (business reports and proposals). For project management, the equivalent basic operating system is process thinking. Specific project management tools and techniques are then used to develop the project outline and more detailed plans and we will come to these in subsequent chapters. For the moment we wish to consider the generality of process thinking and just why it is so important and yet so difficult for many.

Case study

The team met to discuss the implementation of the new payments system. It had to be in place within 9 months and the heat was on to prepare a plan for implementation. It was a very complicated and contentious system. The team rapidly became absorbed in debating the details of the policy and the possible ramifications. The permutations in terms of calculation of reimbursement were mind boggling. It also became very apparent that this change was closely linked with a number of other system changes being considered by other groups. The time moved by and the project manager drew the meeting to a close with a summary of the issues and the linkages with other projects but he was unable to summarise how the group would now proceed.

Process thinking defined

The case is typical of many meetings that dive into the detail of an issue without concluding a way forward. It illustrates the tendency under pressure to work the issues rather than plan the process.

Consider the following questions:

- How would you go about developing a new strategy for your business?

- How would you go about developing a shared employee understanding of the need to make changes in service for customers?

- How would you go about designing the new office accommodation?

- How would you go about improving your team's effectiveness?

The answers to the "how would you go about" questions illustrate what we mean by the term process. Most simply, process is how you work to get something done or resolved. The questions express process thinking. The term embraces such things as:

- **Methodologies/approaches** These are established recipes for achieving a product, a step by step guide to getting something done. For example, a methodology for determining the health needs of a population might be to undertake an assessment of the local demography, to log health issues, to review current services and their effectiveness, to identify gaps and then to develop proposals for filling the gaps. A method for problem solving might be to define the problem specifically, to identify potential causes and then test cause against the observed problem, then moving to the identification of solutions for the most probable cause.

- **Tools and techniques** These will be used within the overall approach or methodology to achieve very specific products. For example, benchmarking and scenario planning and brainstorming are tools and techniques that might be employed at different points within strategic planning.

- **Interventions** This is a term especially used in organisation development to cover ways of working with individuals or groups which leads to insight and learning that can lead to performance improvement. An intervention in a meeting might be to pose a set of reflective questions. A larger scale example would be the design and implementation of a feedback questionnaire, or helping a project team clarify is purpose statement.

Table 6 illustrates typical methodologies and tools or techniques that might be applied in a range of projects.

Process is a logical and sequenced series of steps taking you from A to B. But process is also the set of tools and techniques within these steps.

Illustration of process thinking applied to different kinds of projects

Project Type	Developing a Strategy	Redesigning services	Developing new software	Restructuring
Method Approach	• Examine current state • Consider future environment • Objective setting • Identify options • Model options • Appraise and select	• Review current services and performance • Identify future performance requirements • Re-design process • Model impact on capability and cost • Test with customers • Decide on new design	• Develop specification • Initial design • Beta development • Testing • Revision • Roll out	• Define performance requirements and functions • Identify structure options • Model options for other capability areas • Model for change and investment required • Test models against performance requirement • Select structure
Tools Techniques	• SWOT/PEST analysis • Scenario planning • Gap analysis • Option appraisals	• Process mapping • Benchmarking • Statistical process control/variance analysis	• Customer surveys • Functionality assessments • Value engineering	• Systems thinking • Excellence models • Stakeholder analysis • Force field assessment
People Interventions	• Focus groups • Visioning workshops	• Customer survey • Design workshops	• Simulation events	• Open space/large group • Townhall meetings

Table 6

The illustration in the table highlights two levels of process thinking that we will term high and low levels. The term high level tends to denote conceptual or general thinking, while low level usually refers to specific or practical details. High level thinking will be informed by known methodologies while the low level will be fuelled by specific tools and techniques

High Level Process
High level process is an overview of the key steps required to complete a task. For example, the high level process description for achieving the implementation of a new marketing software programme might be as follows:

1. Development of specification

2. Initial design

3. Beta testing

4. Roll out

Often points of high level definition are used to describe the phases of the project, or key milestones. A specific methodology might determine the high level definition. The steps described above are derived from a standard product development methodology. For construction projects, a design and build approach or methodology has a number of standard high level steps.

Low Level Process

The more detailed low level process definition would entail taking each of the high level steps and working up the detailed actions. For example, the more detailed process for achieving the "Specification" in Step One might be to:

1. Determine customer needs

2. Consolidate needs into outline specification

3. Test the specification

4. Revise

5. Get sign off

Even with this level of definition there are still some "how do you go about" questions. For example, how do you go about determining customer needs? This requires further process thinking to take you into the detail of designing and implementing questionnaires or structured interviews with sample customers. You might employ specific market testing tools and techniques. All of this needs to be considered and factored into detail plans.

The mentality of process planning

The planning of process is very challenging in a number of respects. Firstly, it means abstracting yourself from the specific problems and issues of the project, and devoting time to planning a way forward. Given the pressure on managers and senior staff to obtain results, the general environment may not be conducive to this abstraction. Those who wish to close early on action may be less inclined to tolerate more reflective consideration of the way in which things should be done. The tendency to early closure may be a general cultural inclination within the organisation or it may just reflect individual temperament.

The next challenge lies in the difference between higher level conceptual thinking and more detailed process. It is very unusual for people to have a natural inclination for both. The more intuitive of us are likely to operate at a higher level of thinking and be content with outline plans. More detailed planning assumes an eye for detail.

Summary

Thinking in process terms is at the very heart of good project management. At each stage of the project there is a need to be clear on what you are doing and how you will go about it. Process is simply how you go about working on something to achieve a conclusion. Process thinking embraces two levels of thinking. The higher level comes first and describes the general approach or methodology. Lower level assumes a detail of planning that draws upon tools, techniques and interventions for achieving very specific products. The organisation's culture and your prevailing mentality may prove to underpin or undermine time given to both levels of thinking. But such thinking is key to building confidence in the early stages and in delivering the results in the end.

Now it is your turn

Think about your project and yourself

1. **What kind of project are you trying to deliver? Is it about policy, strategy, service redesign or what?**

2. **Have methodologies or approaches been decided and if so what are they?**

3. **What tools and techniques or interventions could you anticipate using?**

4. **What are your own planning strengths and weaknesses?**

5. **What do you think you may have to learn and develop to become a better planner?**

Chapter Five

Big Picture Thinking

Getting the Project Overview

How will this chapter help you?

The previous chapter provided the basis for project planning with its differentiation of High Level from Low Level thinking. We now want to focus on the High Level thinking that goes into defining why you are doing the project in the first place, what you want to achieve and produce, and what you consider to be the "Big Steps" involved. We call this "Big Picture" thinking. It produces the overall rationale for the project and, when well formed, provides motivation to take the project through its life. Client and team support for a project often hinges on clarity and the vividness of the Big Picture. This chapter will cover what we mean by this thinking and how to achieve it for your project. We start with a case study to illustrate some of the issues.

Case study

> **The Finance Managers from each of the Regional Information Services organisations stared at each other across the table. They knew about the formal appointment of a Global Information Officer. It had been predicted after the success of the Strategy Project. The Board had agreed the strategy, but its implementation now required a global and integrated information services organisation.**
>
> **Today's meeting was key in moving integration forward. Nothing could be achieved without harmonised business planning, project management and financial systems. Harmonisation of these systems fell to the Finance Managers. After a series of presentations from each FM on the current systems employed, it was obvious that a regional organisation had encouraged a proliferation of different approaches. Before long, the meeting descended into the detail of the differences and what to do.**

This example is fairly typical of early encounters on contentious and complex projects. Gripped by anxiety to show progress, participating members quickly take the discussion into details. But early discussions should focus on achieving a strong overview of the project, and address basic questions:

- What is the project about?

- Why are we doing it?

- What is involved – what are the big steps, the approach or method?

Diagram 3 shows the logical sequence of the questions and uses formal project management speak to structure the thinking.

Box 1 – The Business Context sets out in general terms **what has given rise to the project.** In the commercial world this could be a changed financial position that generates a requirement for cost savings or enhanced income. There might have been a particular incident revealing a systems or organisational weakness. Within the public sector it might be a general performance issue or a change in policy. Business context offers us clues as to the origin and drive for the project and gives us a way into the "why are we doing this project" question.

Box 2 – Long Term Outcomes makes explicit the **long term benefits that are expected as a result of the project.** It does not include those things that the project must deliver in the short term. For example, a new building may enable company expansion of services and thus growth in income. It might on the other hand enable the achievement of increased productivity because of the co-location of previously remote staff. The benefits or outcomes of the project will therefore be expressed in terms of increased income or cost savings (or both). This box provides quantitative and qualitative precision on the "why are we doing this project" question.

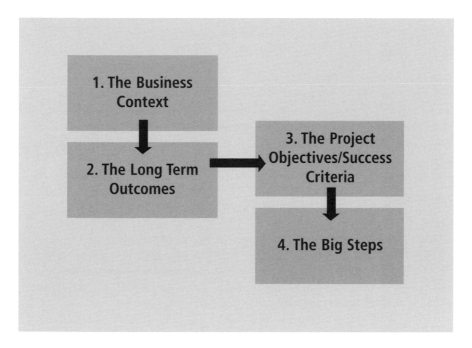

Diagram 3

Box 3 – Project Objectives and Success Criteria concentrates on the **short/medium term deliverables of the project.** In the case of a building project this would include the successful construction and commissioning of the facility. The project manager could not be held accountable for the income and cost position achieved post commissioning, but it would be reasonable to judge the project manager's effectiveness on the basis of successful construction and commissioning of the building. It provides an answer to the "what is this project about" question.

The example begs the issue of exactly what we mean by "successful construction and commissioning of the building" which requires discussion and specification of the broad success criteria for the project. Given that most projects have a time, cost and quality dimension, these elements tend to provide the categories that define the success criteria. The most problematic one is the quality criteria. In terms of the building, it is likely to be one that conforms to the functional specification. For a policy development project, the quality criteria may lie in its clarity, realism and degree of ownership (or commitment) by key stakeholders to the resulting policy.

Box 4 – The Big Steps summarises the **key process steps required to achieve the project's short/medium term objectives.** We looked at this in the previous chapter and you saw how the Big Steps and approach were most often derived from specific methodologies. For the construction of a building one might assume the following:

- Design
- Build
- Commissioning

This "high level" definition says nothing about precise activities, timescales and resourcing. This more detailed definition comes with the second phase of planning. But this high level view does help illuminate the sequence of "what might be involved in the project".

Why are these four boxes or elements so important in the first instance?
It is because they:

- **Provide motivation and encourage energy for the project.** The context and the outcomes (or benefits) provide the overall drive and mission. They may be realised beyond the project terms of reference or life expectancy, but the statement encapsulates the end results and serves as a binding agent for those actively participating in the project or funding it.

- **Provide a boundary for the project with realistic expectations about what the project can and can not deliver.** In project management parlance this is often referred to as project scope having a major influence on the breadth of the activity falling within the project that in turn impacts on the budget required.

- **Offer a broad "balanced scorecard" for the project covering elements of time, cost and quality.** The identification of quality criteria in particular will assist in shaping the activities required within the project. For example, if ownership and commitment are seen as key success criteria for the project, then the project approach and plan will need to build in appropriate processes to engage stakeholders and thus to help secure such ownership.

- **Provide a framework of thinking to establish milestones.** The Big Picture overview helps to establish the Big Steps and therefore define the milestones that can be used to assess overall progress and to ensure that the project is on track.

- **Provide a framework of thinking on which to base more detailed propositions.** The identification of the Big Steps leads logically to the more detailed appraisal of the activities, resources and time required to achieve each one. We tackle this in the next chapter.

Let's go back to the case study cited at the beginning of the chapter.

The **context** for the business planning and financial systems harmonisation lies in the new Information Strategy developed for the Company which in turn calls for greater uniformity of trading systems, quicker and more customer focussed development, with lower costs of ownership for technology and systems. A key requirement of the strategy is to have one integrated Information Services organisation.

This project is focussed on the **delivery** of harmonised Information Services planning and control systems, including financial management of systems development and operations maintenance work. This is to enable one Information Services organisation to operate effectively and, through this, to obtain in the longer term the advantages of lower cost of technology and speed of systems development for users.

The **success criteria** for the project will be the delivery of harmonised systems within the time specified and within an agreed budget. Important quality criteria for the project will be conformity to the specifications of the new Chief Information Officer and their team. Other important criteria may be migration cost from current systems, and minimal risk management within the project in terms of loss of productivity around current work programmes and commitments.

At a high level, the approach or method will cover the following **Big Steps**:

1. Review of current systems within the current regional organisations

2. Outline specification for new systems

3. Agreement on development priorities

4. Detailed design by priority

5. Test of systems

6. Implementation planning

7. Implementation

Summary

There are basic questions that should be answered at the outset of a project. What is the context for our project? What are we trying to achieve in the long term? What must be delivered in the short term? What are the Big Steps involved? The Big Picture, or high level thinking, is key to securing support and motivation for the project from clients and from those helping with delivery. Established methodologies may well suggest or dictate the Big Steps involved. These Big Steps provide a framework for establishing milestones and the more detailed plan. It also enables an approach for the higher level performance management of the project.

Now it is your turn!

Think of your project and answer the following questions:

1. **What has given rise to your project? What are the starting problems or contextual issues?**

2. **What long term outcomes are intended as a result of the project?**

3. **What must your project deliver in the short term? What are the broader success criteria?**

4. **What established methodologies are there for this kind of project? What Big Steps are involved?**

Chapter Six

Detailed Project Planning

How will this chapter help you?

We now move from the Big Picture into the detail. This is where the reality of a project confronts the project manager. What precisely must be done by whom and when? How much will everything cost? When will the project be delivered? Detailed thinking is essential in testing the reality of client expectations and agreeing a realistic contract. Without sufficient or accurate detail, project managers may over promise and put themselves and the project at risk from the start. This chapter aims to provide the essential thinking tools to get to the detail and enable you to estimate and make the case for the right level of resource. We start with an overview of the process.

In Diagram 4 you can see that the detailed thinking feeds off the Big Picture thinking described in the previous chapter. The link is the Big Steps box.

Overview of the Detailed Project Planning Process

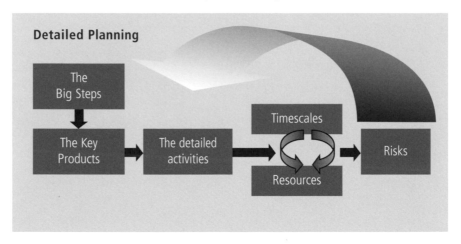

Diagram 4

The process is:

> 1. **Converting the Big Steps into a series of "products"**
>
> 2. **Taking each product and drilling down to define the tools/techniques and actions required to deliver that product**
>
> 3. **Considering what each activity entails and the level of interdependency between activities**
>
> 4. **Estimating the resource needed for each activity and therefore estimating how long the activity will take**

5. Finally turning the thinking on its head and considering what could go wrong so as to improve the plan.

Let us illustrate the application of this process via a case study.

Case study

It was an unusual sight. Uniformed Prison Officers sitting around the table for the first time with non uniformed health managers and professionals. They spoke a different language. One group talked of "lock ups" and "fitting out "whilst the other spoke of "co-morbidity and health status". But they were there to undertake a joint project with a very clear focus on delivery. Even the methodology was provided. However, they only had 8 weeks to complete the project and they needed to be structured and organised.

The Prison Health Needs Assessment Project required the completion of a review of health needs and services with proposals on change within 8 weeks. The review had to be based on best information and evidence and owned by the Prison Governor and leaders of health organisations. This is the statement of **delivery objective and success criteria**. The needs assessment the project will produce would be a major milestone in a longer term project, delivering improved health services and thus improved health for the prison population. These are the **outcomes and benefits** of the work.

The **methodology** was also clear. To achieve a completed assessment the following activities needed to be undertaken by the project group:

1. A review of health problems that would make clear the general health issues for the prison population and the scale of the problem and its consequences

2. A baseline review of health services making clear what was being provided by whom and to what standard

3. Review of evidence and best practice achieved elsewhere to treat or manage these health conditions

4. Recommendations on health improvement targets and priorities for service and organisation investment

5. A provisional action plan with specification of finance required

These activities give a sense of what is involved in the project and constitute the "Big Steps". We now need to drill down into each area and understand precisely how they will be undertaken.

At this stage, we take each of the Big Steps and describe them as products in their own right. The conversion of the list above into products looks like this:

1. The assessment of health problems

2. Baseline assessment of services

3. Recommendations from best practice

4. Recommended improvement targets and priorities

5. Provisional action plan

This may appear something of a presentational play, but it is more than this. We begin to look along the length of the project and describe products coming off the production line that contribute to the overall result. These will later become the milestones that will define the measures for keeping a check on the project's interim progress.

One further element is to consider the relationship of the products to each other. This is important since these relationships will have impact on the overall time required for overall project completion. If we consider the 5 products above, you could deduce that Product 4 is dependent upon having achieved 1, 2 and 3 and product 5 could not be achieved without having delivered 4. However, products 1, 2 and 3 are not dependent upon each other and if we assume that they are not competing for staff time, then we could see the kind of relationship set out in Diagram 5.

Now we need to clamber around in each box and understand precisely how each of these products will be derived. We need to identify the precise tools and techniques that will be needed and describe the activities.

For service review and improvement projects such as the Prison Health case, there is a wide range of analytical tools and techniques that could be used. Benchmarking, process mapping, statistical process control, customer survey techniques, and option appraisal are all likely to be deployed in the work. Each of the techniques involves information gathering, then analysis, which leads to conclusions on what to do next. It is very "left brain" analytical activity which uses logical and rational consideration to uncover elements of the problem and which informs final conclusions and decisions.

The case project will lead to major changes in how staff work to deliver health services. Some of these changes will be contentious and success will be a function of the extent to which staff feel committed and engaged in the process. We will say more about the

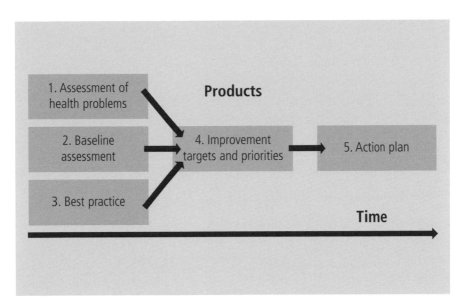

Diagram 5

psychology of change later in the book. The commitment and engagement issue requires a different set of "people interventions" from the analytical tools used to assess the date. These range from large group processes such as open space, whole system planning events, to workshops and focus groups, to task forces, design teams and the like. Effective selection of process is dependent upon identification of the key players, assessment of the best way to inform and engage them, and the trade off between time and involvement. This methodology is focussed on "right brain" considerations around people, their motivation to change, and what they need to change.

Take the **second product** in the Prison Health Needs Assessment Project, the **Baseline Review of Services**. The assessment of strengths and weaknesses of any service requires the following kind of detailed activity:

1. Agreement on how to categorise and map current services

2. Process mapping of services

3. Identification of key quality and efficiency measures

4. Agreement on information required to assess services

5. Gathering of quantitative information on current services

6. Qualitative survey information on service by customers

7. Benchmark data on best performing units elsewhere in terms of quality and efficiency

8. Data consolidation

9. Data analysis

10. Conclusions on strengths and weaknesses (Achieving the Product)

Commitment and credibility issues require thinking about who must be involved in the information gathering and analysis. In this case, prisoners, Board of Visitors, managers, healthcare staff and those who audit and inspect prisons may be seen to be key to the successful assessment. Then, the issue becomes one of the most effective way of engaging these parties. For a customer view of service, individual prisoner survey and focus groups are likely to be a useful technique in providing data for the assessment. To heighten the impact on those who provide service, the assessments might be taped and relayed to groups of providers to hear and discuss. Visits by health staff to other establishments may bring alive the benchmarked data on service comparisons. Data consolidation and presentation of crude un-interpreted data in workshop mode might be the best way of getting staff to get to grips with and to internalise the conclusions and messages.

So the technical and commitment considerations will inform the detailed activity plan. The next question focuses on the order in which these activities should be undertaken. Two considerations prevail; the first requires thinking about the relationship of inputs to outputs. The second consideration looks at the dependency of activities on the same resources, often staff time. In taking the first consideration we could draw up the following representation of the tasks and their relationship.

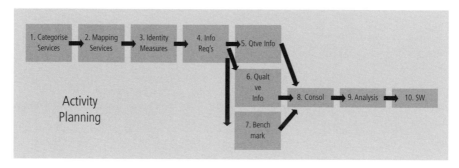

Diagram 6 – Using activities listed on Page 57

We can see that tasks 1 to 4 require working sequentially because there is an input and output sequence; you can't do 2 without having completed 1. But when you come to tasks 5, 6 and 7, these could be done in parallel because they are not dependent upon each other. However, task 8 is dependent upon the successful completion of 5, 6 and 7. Tasks 9 and 10 show dependencies on prior activities. Software programmes will automatically ask in the build up of dependencies for the task dependencies. Now let's consider the issue of resources constraints. If tasks 5, 6 and 7 depended on the 100% use of the same staff members then you would have to separate these and show them sequentially.

More Process Thinking

There is, however, still a requirement for more process thinking. As you look at the first three tasks, you could think of a number of ways of gaining clarity on the categorisation of services, of process mapping them and finally agreeing quality and efficiency measures. Perhaps all three could be done within a single workshop comprising the key service providers. Doing it this way, in a workshop could serve also to inform and engage service providers, and increase their involvement in the project and their interest or commitment to the project outcome. If this is the right approach then consideration will need to be given to a date, a venue and pre session communication. There will be a judgement about whether to brief attendees prior to the meeting or whether to start with a clean sheet of paper. There will always be a trade off in projects between speed of movement and degree of involvement and commitment obtained.

Whichever process you select, the detail of your thinking needs to go into the activity plan. This may extend the time frame but hopefully the results will be more robust.

Another judgement you must make is about the amount of time it will take you to undertake each activity. This will be dependent upon who does the work, their level of skill and capability, their availability and who else they need to work with.

For some projects, a proportion of the work might be contracted out of the organisation. In this case your role as project manager may well involve procurement and overall performance management of work done by external suppliers. Detailed activity planning will form the basis of the contractor's proposals and you will be part of the negotiation process at the front end.

Let us assume, however, that your project is not capital intensive and the resource is essentially made up of internal staff. Against each activity you will need to carefully consider the technical and managerial skill required to achieve each work activity. The big question is how long will the work take? You may be able to estimate this or it may be that you will reach an estimate together with the designated staff members. Either way it is a test of imagination covering the time to:

- Set up the work

- Start the work

- Wait for inputs to be assembled from others doing their bits

- Do other work outside of the project (but that will get in the way of progress on the project)

- Complete the work

This total time for any job will be the **duration**, that is, **the total time for**

completing the task including an allowance for down time. As an example, if a key project activity is writing a report, the actual writing might take 6 hours, but if this is scheduled in a week where a staff member cannot devote 6 straight hours, then you may have to accept a total time for the task of 2 days. This is the duration or elapsed time not the actual time on the report.

Let's summarise where we are in the detailed planning phase. Detailed project planning is a cascade of thinking that starts with the Big Steps identified in the Big Picture. We take the Steps as products and then examine each for the process and detailed activity. We assess the relationship of activities in terms of their dependencies. Finally we think about resourcing and how long each activity will take, the duration. Duration is often a gut feel about how long a task takes given levels of skill and productivity. Total duration or elapsed time builds in waits and distractions to provide the total time from start to finish for a job, Big Step or the project as a whole.

The thinking comes together in a Gantt chart as below.

ID	Task Name	Duration	Start	26 Jan '04							02 Feb '04		
				M	T	W	T	F	S	S	M	T	W
1	**Assessment of current services**	**26 days**	Fri 30/01/04										
2	Agree template and approach	1 day	Fri 30/01/04								Andy/Richard/Le		
3	Gather prison data	3 days	Mon 02/02/04										
4	Gather data on NHS provision	9 days	Mon 02/02/04										
5	Gather benchmark data	15 days	Mon 02/02/04										
6	Develop census approach	1 day	Mon 02/02/04										
7	Test approach	5 days	Tue 03/02/04										
8	Set up census activity	5 days	Tue 10/02/04										
9	Undertake census	10 days	Tue 17/02/04										
10	First cut of information	3 days	Fri 13/02/04										
11	Initial conclusions	3 days	Wed 18/02/04										

Diagram 7

Line one of the grid shows the Product at the Big Step level (Assessment of Current Services) and lines 2 onwards show the activities required to achieve the product with durations and start dates. The total duration of the product is seen as 26 days, that is the summation of all detailed activity and individual activity durations.

Project costs are always an issue in working environments that require careful assessment at the business case stage when the decision will be made whether to proceed with projects or not. We saw in the Big Picture discussion how the benefits of the project provide the basis for some quantification of the return for investment. These might be calculated on the basis of income generated or costs saved.

The costs of the project come from the detailed product and activity planning, and assumptions made about resources required, whether they be internal or external. For the kinds of projects that we are envisaging, the costs will be predominantly found in staff time devoted to the project activity. Therefore, a crude costing may be derived from taking forecasted hours spent on activities or products at agreed staff hourly rates. There are likely to be other areas of fixed and variable project costs. Fixed costs would include those associated with the project management office. Variable costs might include special events for the project (workshops, training etc.) and time spent at regular group meetings (Steering Group/Project Group meetings) as well as the costs of work associated with each activity.

It is not our purpose to take the issue of costing any further and, frankly, it would be better to consult your internal financial managers on requirements for costing and appraisal of projects.

One final checking process on project realism and viability is the **risk assessment**.

The key risk assessment questions at this early point in project planning are:

- **What could go wrong with our plan?**
- **How likely are the problems to occur and if they do, what real impact would they have on the plan and its achievement?**
- **Could we prevent the problem or problems?**
- **What would we do if the problems occur?**

Having laboured to produce the detail of the plan and its resourcing, it is hard then to contemplate failure or difficulty. At this stage most motivated people want simply to get on with the job in hand; undue optimism may prevail. The risk assessment is designed to provoke reflection on what has been agreed and to test the thinking for the assumptions made. The most rigorous test is normally achieved using a group comprised of those intimately involved with the planning and those who might be coming afresh to the thinking.

Kepner-Tregoe's Potential Problem Analysis (PPA) (Kepner and Tregoe, 1997; Longman and Mullins, 2005) offers a systematic approach to the assessment of risks and action planning to manage them effectively. Their process begins with looking at the plan, and for each main activity and sub activities, brainstorming potential problems that could arise. Each problem is then assigned a level of probability of occurrence (using high, medium and low) and a level of impact if it does occur (using the same high medium and low probability). Problems that seem likely to occur and to be disruptive are further analysed to identify likely causes. Preventive actions are identified for the most likely causes. Against the same problems, contingency actions are defined that could be taken to minimise the impact should the problem actually occur. The final step of this process is to analyse the preventive and contingency actions for costs and effort, and then build the approved contingency actions into the original action plan.

You can see that the critical piece of analysis hinges around the assessment of probability and impact of potential problems.

In our case study, one major problem identified from the outset was the risk of partial availability of information on service activity and quality of service. Much of the information was manually collected and did not cover services comprehensively. The absence of data would seriously undermine the eventual assessment of problems and priorities for change so it was decided to undertake a number of sample surveys of service on given days of the week. If for any reason the surveys were insufficient, use would be made of a one off review of service undertaken some 12 months previously.

Using the structure of the risk assessment tool, we see the following:

- The problem was the availability of information on service use and quality

- The probability was very high (given current data capture processes) and the consequence to the outcome of the project was high (it would undermine the assessment of current service deficiencies)

- The preventive action (to prevent non availability of information) was to set up a series of surveys

- The contingent action was to utilise the previous one off audit of service undertaken 12 months ago.

Summary

Detailed Project Planning begins with the Big Steps outlined in the Big Picture project overview. The Big Steps are then seen as products. Detailed Planning establishes the tools, techniques and activities to achieve each product. Activities may be undertaken in parallel or sequentially, depending upon the interdependencies. Each activity will assume a given level of input and thus time and cost and there may be trade offs between cost and the time for delivery. A push to progress the project quickly normally means putting more staff on the job, and that effectively increases the cost to the project. The resulting plan is finally submitted to a risk assessment that fundamentally means turning the thinking on its head to assess the potential problems. The result should be an improved plan.

Now it is your turn!

Think of your project and answer the following questions:

1. What are the Big Steps?

2. How would you describe these in product terms?

Take one of the products

1. What tools and techniques will you use to achieve a quality product?

2. What activities are assumed?

3. How long will each activity take and how much staff or other input is assumed

4. If you had to lay out the activities on a time line, what would this look like? (which activities are dependent on other activities, which are not?)

5. Is the overall timing of product delivery acceptable to you? Is the overall cost of the activity acceptable to you?

6. If the overall timescale is not acceptable, what appear to be the key activities determining the overall timescale? What could be done to speed them up? What would be the cost of doing this?

7. What problems might you anticipate? What is your assessment of the probability and the consequence?

8. What preventive and contingency actions should you build into your plan at this stage?

Chapter Seven

Change and Project Management

How will this chapter help you?

We stated in our opening chapter that change is an intrinsic part of any project. Projects that produce new buildings, processes or strategies at some point require change in the way in which people behave and perform. Bringing about behavioural change is tricky. For as many reasons as we may be drawn to new futures, there will be countervailing forces rooting us in the past. We can work hard to get the building up on time, but we can not be sure that people will work in the new integrated way we had hoped. There has been much written on the psychology of change that helps the Project Manager understand what is important and how to deploy appropriate processes to engage and help move people forward.

This chapter aims to set out some practical approaches to integrating the notion of successful change management into your project. We start with an overview of common problems in thinking about change. Then we set out an approach built around theories of how individuals and groups react and respond to externally imposed change, whilst adapting to change themselves. We'll ask you to apply the thinking to your project, and in the following chapter show how the thinking applies to our own case study.

Why traditional project management thinking may not be enough

The previous chapters (Big Picture and more Detailed Project Planning) set out the requirements for clarity on what we are trying to achieve and how we propose to proceed. The approach is rational, logical and structured, and the eventual plan provides comfort for managing an uncertain future. The thinking tends to emphasise the positive; it also focuses on those things that can be mechanistically planned and executed. Difficult and challenging "people changes", those that rely on human adaptation or learning, are often underplayed or addressed in rather mechanistic ways.

Here are just three examples of the limitations of traditional thinking:

- **The project terms of reference are too narrow and do not link with other changes.** A good example of this is normally found in IT projects. A new computer system may well provide the technical platform for an integration of sales and manufacturing effort and lead to improved efficiency; but we know that the achievement of efficiencies will be dependent upon changes at the end of the day in how staff relate and work together. The new computer system will help, but other changes will be needed, for example changes in work location, general communication, roles and responsibilities. The solution needs to take the IT technical development as part of a bigger change programme sharing a common business drive. The alternative is to widen the terms of reference and goals of the IT project to take on board the broader change issues.

- **Project activity plans do not make provision for processes that are needed to ensure engagement, acceptance and commitment to new ways of doing things.** The activity plan for the design, beta testing and implementation of a new computer system may well emphasise steps in its technical development, but does not build in engagement processes to ensure understanding, ownership and widespread use by the staff it's been designed to assist.

- **Risk assessments do not take account of predictable issues of resistance to change.** A system requiring new integrated ways of working may cut across existing structures that currently offer stability of work and relationships. People can resist this for all kinds of understandable reasons. Such resistance can slow down implementation or make it ultimately ineffective. An experienced change manager will be able to anticipate reactions that accompany contentious change and be able to design in actions to head off or use the tension constructively.

It is our mission in this chapter to help you make your plans more comprehensive, not for the sake of pristine bureaucracy but because such thinking should make a substantial difference to achieving the changes you desire.

Thinking about the nature of change within your project and the tools of change management

Have a look at the following illustrations of different ways of thinking about a new production facility project.

- **Project Goal A:** To ensure the design and construction of the new production facility on time, to cost and meeting certain functional requirements
- **Project Goal B:** To ensure improvements in employee productivity on the basis of the new production facility

Both definitions refer to the new production facility and on this basis, you would expect to see an approach and detailed plan that covers the mechanics of design and construction of a new facility. However, in the second definition, we see the project framed so that it emphasises the new facility and includes other initiatives designed to enable new working methods and ultimately new levels of productivity.

> **The way in which scope, objectives and success criteria are framed shape how you plan and approach the project.**

Diagram 8 below illustrates the Project Goal B, and the kind of thinking that we consider key to effecting change.

The illustration takes the end goals as being the achievement of new behaviour and performance. It makes clear that both "Design and Construction" and "Other Capability Changes" are "means" to the intended Behaviour and Performance objectives. The capability workstream could embrace changes in job design and organisation of work, payment and communication systems with supporting education and training programmes.

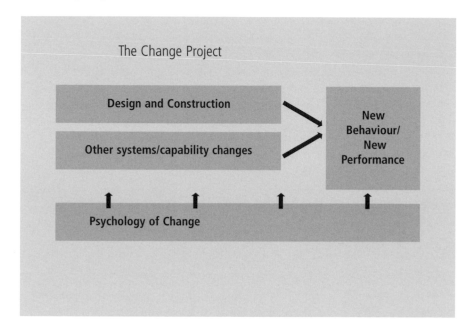

Diagram 8

We know that a key ingredient to bringing change about successfully will be a shift in mentalities and attitudes to support new behaviour and performance. The underlying Psychology of Change is not a box of programmable activity, but rather a dynamic, shifting state of opinion, beliefs and attitudes that work for or against the desired changes. As project managers we can influence these factors, but we cannot require them. The tools of influence lie in the change management toolbox that we will examine at the end of the chapter before the case study.

A General Approach to Change Management
In the study of economics, it is difficult to understand the working of economies without appreciating the market behaviour of individual firms. It is the same for change management. Understanding the dynamics of change for individuals helps with building a change strategy for groups and organisations.

The Nature of Change and Individual Response
The American change consultant, William Bridges, distinguishes between changes in the environment and deeper more personal change.

Over a lifetime, we will experience a number of so called environmental changes: new jobs, homes, partners and life styles. Psychological dynamics influence how we actually behave in these new situations, testing the degree to which we really embrace new identities, values and beliefs, as we make a transition from "old" living to "new". Some changes in environment assume significant personal change. For example, settling with a partner assumes a new shared identity with a degree of sustained common interest. This generally means giving up some things we used to do on our own or with old friends. Failure to do this may undermine the relationship and its longevity.

The same is true of change that we experience in organisational life. The first promotion from a technical position to a managerial one requires real shifts in what we do day to day. We move off some of the technical detail and begin to manage a process involving other people. We begin to plan and organise and rely on others to execute. We have a new identity for ourselves and learn to value achieving through others. Failure to make this transition can mean doing the work as well as managing, leading to personal overload and seriously demotivated staff.

The Psychology of Change – Making Successful Transitions

A good deal of the research on the reactions of people to change comes from studies associated with illness and death. In clinical settings, the focus was on the patterns of reactions to changes or to diagnostic information that changed the patient's or family's life. Put very briefly, it was concluded that it was possible to anticipate a predictable (if not inevitable) trajectory of reactions from shock, denial, anger, guilt, remorse, depression through to resignation and acceptance, and then often a readiness to face the future. Grief and loss are key psychological elements.

Reactions to change in work life can follow similar patterns and this predictability can help project managers plan for change.

William Bridges focuses on the psychological phases that people experience. He outlines three phases:

- **Endings** where there is active contemplation of loss be it in terms of jobs or activities, relationships, status, identity or skills. This contemplation may be accompanied by an array of feelings ranging from shock, anger and resistance to resignation and the desire to negotiate change. It can also be that the endings are greeted with relief and some enthusiasm.

- **A neutral zone** where the certainties of the past are left behind, but where the future is not yet clear. It is a period characterised by unease, uncertainty and anxiety.

- **New beginnings** where changes take root and new patterns, jobs and routines become established. Life is much clearer. For many this is the dawn arrival, exciting and refreshing, but for others it is a dawning realisation of change and may evoke a holding on to the old rather than embrace of the new.

Bridges makes the point that these are not sequential stages and that for many, the ability to say goodbye to old routines will require the confidence of successful experimentation and the security of success during the new beginnings. It is also clear that for those who are keen to embrace change, the movement through phases may be rapid.

The issue of resistance often dominates change literature, but we do not have to assume that such response is inevitable. For some, the prospect of change may offer a real opportunity to break from a dissatisfying current situation. The personal benefits may be obvious and individuals may feel very confident about the future based on positive prior experience or inherent confidence in their own abilities.

For others, change may prove daunting and disruptive. It may mean new duties, assuming new skills or patterns of work and relationships. There may be an underlying fear of not coping with the new environment. There may be deep feelings of loss of identity as sources of power, influence, status and relationships change with new organisational arrangements. Moreover, there may be feelings of loss of control of destiny and the future, as individuals feel victims of change being driven at them. Such feelings can be manifested in behaviour that is loosely termed "resistance". But resistance can take diverse forms ranging from avoidance and detachment to argument and conflict.

Personality and Change

A final perspective on individuals and change comes with the study of personality and behaviour. In particular we are interested in understanding:

- What causes stress for individuals in times of change

- What kind of information is likely to assist individuals in making change

- What kind of involvement individuals need in the change process

The Myers Briggs Type Inventory (Briggs Myers and Myers, 1995) is used by many organisations to develop empathy and sensitivity to differences in personality. The Inventory looks at the following:

- An individual's orientation towards extraversion or introversion, where individuals derive their source of energy. Extraverts being more expressive whilst introverts are more reflective and inward.

- The degree to which individuals process ideas on the basis of concrete observations and information (sensing), emphasising the past and present, as opposed to a more intuitive process (intuition) emphasising future possibilities.

The difference is between gathering more detailed information on the need for change and the proposals as opposed to "running with ideas".

- The predisposition of individuals to take decisions in a very analytical and systematic way (thinking) as opposed to decision making using values and beliefs with a high concern for the impact on people (feeling)

- The orientation of individuals towards closing on propositions (judging) as opposed to keeping options open and flexible (perceiving)

Individual preferences in each of the dimensions produces an intricate overall personality type that has impact on the kind of information that an individual feels he needs and the preferred process for working on and through issues. There are clear differences for each of the dimensions:

- Extraverts want to engage in early and active discussion on the future whilst introverts need time and space to reflect on propositions and to make sense of them

- Sensing types want more detail on the change propositions and want to understand their connection with the past. Intuitive types are much more at ease with general propositions preferring to engage quickly in developing possibilities for the future

- Thinking types need to be assured of the credibility and competence of others and their decisions. They look for clear logical analysis. Feeling types need to understand how change fits with important underlying values and principles; they want to ensure that the impact on people is fully understood and is worked properly

- Judging types look for form and structure in plans for change where perceiving types wish to ensure that options are not closed off prematurely.

Generally predictable sources of stress for individuals during change include:

- A lack of information on what is going on

- An inability to influence the pace of change and the propositions themselves

- A pace of change that does not allow for reflection and assimilation

- Propositions that confront all that they hold dear and make no sense

- A lack of support to understand and then master new situations, a feeling of developing incompetence

- Feeling alienated from people and isolated

- Plans that are too open ended and do not provide certainty

Type Theory helps us to recognise that the cause of stress will be different for different personalities. For example, stress for some will be the feeling of being over controlled by others with insufficient opportunity to shape futures (the intuitive types). For others, it is the absence of detail that confronts their sense of history and loyalty or their ability to really grasp the appeal of the new (the sensing and thinking types). It may be the lack of time and space for reflection (introverts), or the inability to move quickly into discussions on possible futures (the extravert intuitives).

Practical implications of Type Theory are that different types require different kinds of information (detail versus outline) and different ways of engaging (for example experiential workshops versus good written communication). It may be impossible to design processes to respond to the vast array of different needs all at the same time, but a good change programme will aim to provide a mix of communication and information modes that take into account different preferences.

Summary

Before we move on to consider change management as applied to groups, let us summarise the key points so far.

- Changes in environment do not automatically produce change in individual behaviour

- Personal transition takes place as individuals pass through different psychological states; individuals make transitions at different rates

- Some in the organisation will champion change and some will resist

- Resistance is not always obvious

- Reactions to change such as anxiety, fear and exhilaration may be learned behaviour build up on the basis of previous experience of change

- Much anxiety is caused by feelings of being out of control or the victim of change

- Different personality types need different information and involvement processes

Applying change principles to groups and organisations

There are two further theories or approaches that may help your thinking about change for groups. The first is a way of thinking about phases of change and the second is an amalgam of experience based on empirical evidence.

Quite amazingly, Kurt Lewin's classic model (Lewin, 1948, 1951), which schematised distinct phases of movement in beliefs and behaviour over time in situations of change, still serves project and change management thinking and planning :

- **Unfreezing** where the organisation and its people can see, acknowledge and accept the need for change

- **Mobilising** where people become energised around the prospects of change and begin to experiment and explore new routines

- **Refreezing** where the organisation actually put binding around new patterns of behaviour through structure, process and reward.

There is no direct connection between these phases and Bridge's phases of transition, but they do offer another way of thinking about a progression of change activity helping to move from old to new.

Management consultants and business school academics put their money behind a recipe of process that builds understanding and commitment and moves the organisation forward. The processes are geared to meeting individual and collective needs for reassurance and certainty on the direction of travel and the journey. But they also seek to achieve momentum and delivery.

Case studies on change suggest the following key ingredients are key to successful change management:

- **A compelling case** for change that is understood and becomes the overriding corporate logic for change. The case should be rooted in the outside world providing an external rather than internal requirement for change in performance to ensure customer and shareholder return. **Within the case for change, we should be clear about what will happen if the organisation fails to move**.

- **A vision for change** that offers meaningful and attractive propositions of the future. The vision of change looks forward to the medium or longer term describing the characteristics and shape of products and services as well as organisational capabilities (structure, process, skills, competencies and culture/style). Initially these visions may be a very high and general level. There may be a tendency to devote more time to clarifying the vision for the organisation than the product and service output. **Having a vision of project output is essential because it provides legitimacy for organisational change propositions**. For the more prolonged and complicated change projects there will also need to be a vision of transition, that describes the pace and scale of change over time.

- **Clarity on process** Being clear and open on what is going to happen and when, serves to ease what might be genuine uncertainty for individuals. The change process can cover various phases, starting with clarity on the case for change, moving to outline, and on to more detailed changes. Because actual implementation may be months away (which can be unsettling or even destabilising), clarity on the process and timing of phases and of decisions is critical in helping to manage the uncertainty around individual and corporate futures.

- **Effective pacing of change** that ensures momentum in terms of environmental change but which also acknowledges the need for psychological adjustment. The pacing of change will hinge around senior management decisions on the degree of urgency for movement and the degree to which a top down or more participative change process will be applied. We come back to this later in the chapter.

- **Active coalitions** of key stakeholders or sponsors who can provide support and drive for change. We know that some people will help drive change and some will not. Spotting the champions in the early stage is vital. These individuals need to have credibility and influence within the organisation, even though they may not necessarily start with enthusiasm and commitment.

- **Processes of Engagement** that invites enquiry, discussion and contribution, and seeks to engender a broader sense of ownership for change. The corollary of this is not opening up debate on issues where there is a starting "given" or where there are aspects that are non negotiable.

- **Communication processes** that support the key phases of change. While often linked to engagement processes, communication processes are distinct. The underlying objectives of communication strategy hinge on the desire to inform, educate and influence behaviour rather than necessarily build strong and broadly based commitment. The importance of good communication processes is highlighted in virtually all change management models.

We would like to say more on the issues of engagement and communication.

Engagement
Active engagement of people in change environments is much more than just keeping them informed.

Stakeholders, whether internal or external, can be actively engaged in diagnosing current problems and building solutions with the advantage that they feel a greater sense of ownership and responsibility for taking things forward. There exists now a huge array of methods for engaging stakeholders – from large scale group meetings and workshops to more carefully orchestrated project based working.

Large scale group meetings have become a key tool in many organisations where there is a need for insight and bite on change across a system. Large group meetings widen the circle of involvement and enable connection to be made which might not be made otherwise. The actual design of these meetings can take into account the phase of change (e.g. unfreezing, mobilising or refreezing) and draw upon a range of group processes and techniques designed to assist understanding of issues, to enable creativity in problem solving or the recognition of achievements to cement new ways of doing things.

Examples of the different focus for events within the phases are shown below:

Unfreezing	Mobilising	Re-freezing
• The review of customer survey data • The review of benchmarked competitor data • Joint environmental scanning and scenario building	• Vision building • Process design work • Option building and appraisal • Planning	• Recognition of endings • Review of performance and achievements • Learning and development

Large group meetings can involve from 50 to 200 persons or more. These meetings are carefully structured and the process will be driven by clear objectives and outputs, combined with sensitivity to the complexity of the content and the different needs and styles of participants. Designing the varied activities and forms of communication for an event is the way to accommodate the different preferences of personality types described earlier. An event design might include the following:

- Presentation of data for the sensing and analytical types

- Paired or trio reflections for the more introverted and reflective

- Vision building for the more extroverted intuitive and value driven individuals

- Detailed implementation planning for the sensing, analytical and closing types

Communication

An active engagement strategy aims to directly involve others in shaping and driving change, It seeks to distribute leadership broadly within the organisation. The objectives of general communication are different; they are to inform and influence opinion and attitudes while not necessarily inviting input to the change design. Such a one-way approach may well apply in fast moving situations, or where there is an emphasis on top down driven change. The objectives of communication planning can fit with the phased approach described above. For example:

Unfreezing	Mobilising	Re-freezing
Communication emphasis on why we need to change and what happens if we don't	Communication emphasis on the direction, the journey and how to be involved	Communication on what has been achieved, with recognition of learning and individual contribution

Communications planning should be subject to the same kind of rigour expected of the main project plan. This means being clear on:

- **The communication objectives.** Clarity of purpose is important for the communication plan as a whole, for each phase of communication and for each individual communication initiative or activity. In one-way communication, the objectives may be to raise levels of understanding, buy-in and acceptance; in two way communications, using dialogue or feedback loops, the objective may be to seek acknowledgement, recognition and reaction to ideas and concerns, or, contribution in the form of suggestions to the work.

- **The key audiences.** Segmentation of the audience and an understanding of the needs of different groups are key to successful communication. Segmentation may be approached using a number of differentiators: the extent to which a group can impact the change, the roles that groups may play, respective constituencies and geographical distribution, differing social groupings or cultural subsets.

- **The mix of communication processes and channels.** Communication strategies must address the relative merits of:

  o Face to face versus written

  o Interactive (meetings, electronic chat rooms) versus non interactive (large group presentations, written or e-mailed briefings)

  o Conventional hard copy documentation versus electronic

  o Established communication vehicles versus investment in the new

  o The formal (meetings, briefings, reports) versus the informal networks (identifying and using opinion formers)

- **The key communication players and their skill development.** Identification of key personnel with responsibilities for communications is important at the outset. Good communication is labour intensive, so investment in the communication skills and the staff to help formulate and disseminate information are both crucial given that a range of methods may be required (oral presentations, facilitation and discussion leading, memo, newsletter or report writing).

The approach to communication channels and media should mirror the general approach taken in the project. So, if cross organisation group work is being used to disrupt normal working arrangements in order to break historic patterns of behaviour, then the communications channels should mirror and reinforce this. This will mean investing in new processes rather than using traditional line structures. If one of the key themes of the project is achieving modernised service processes, then the communications media should reflect this.

Communication and engagement are very practical manifestations of change management within projects. Therefore, you would expect to see that project plans address both issues in some detail, making provision for the setting up and running of meetings and events, as well as the preparation and dissemination of information.

Underlying management philosophies of change management

The difference between general communication and active engagement is symptomatic of two contrasting management philosophies in managing change. These are often referred to in short hand by the terms "top-down" and "bottom-up".

There will always be a choice in the approach to be taken. The judgement hinges on what has been seen to have worked in the past (cultural issues) and what past experience suggests about success in future. There are important issues of timing and degrees of urgency for change. A key determining factor, however, will be the experience, learning and temperament of the managers themselves combined with their interpretation of the urgency for the achievement of change. Some will lean towards a top down, prescribed approach of change, whilst others may be more facilitative and developmental, preferring consultative direction on what has to be achieved, leaving room for interpretation and evolution of how the desired achievements will be secured.

The differences between the two will be manifested in pace of change and degrees of involvement. Another difference will be in the weight given to various enablers of change; that is the relative use of hard wire enablers like organisational structure and material incentives, versus softer more supportive learning and developmental processes.

Their research on the nature of corporate change, lead Beer and Nohria (2000) to draw two archetypes, or theories of change, that embody the assumptions made by senior executives, and the consultative and academics who advise them, about how and why changes should be made.

Theory E, based on economic values, is characterised as "hard", and produces change programmes that are fast paced and driven by critical and urgent external performance requirements. Shareholder value is held to be the only legitimate means of success. Change is much more top down with an emphasis on major restructuring of businesses, rapid change in key players with extensive use made of personal incentives. Theory E change programmes have a formality of planning and orchestration, with use made of knowledge based consultants to assist in shaping and driving propositions.

Theory O is change based on organisational capacity. The approach is more evolutionary with a higher degree of participation in design and implementation of change. The focus is on developing organisational (hence O), cultural and human capability with a slower and more gradual impact on corporate performance. Where external consultants are used, there are fewer of them and they work in support of a process with less content expertise.

Looking at change programmes in difference organisations, the authors concluded that it is by effectively combining hard and soft approaches to change, that an organisation can equip its staff to increase profitability and production in sustainable ways. There are interesting examples of organisations that have effectively combined both approaches but over different phases.

The tools of Change Management

We turn finally to the practical end of the change management process to set out the key tools and techniques that might be employed during the life of the project. Previously (see chapter on the Challenge of Project Management) we categorised these tools under the two headings of analysis and engagement.

Analysis

These are the tools to help with an analysis of the current and changing state of the organisation and to help in planning effective change strategies and specific interventions. These tools will help with addressing the following key change questions:

- How are we doing now as an organisation?
- Why do we need to change?
- What if we don't change?
- What is the prevailing internal climate of opinions and beliefs and is this conducive to making change?
- Who might be the champions and who might resist change?
- What is our vision of change in service terms?
- What does this vision mean in terms of our organisation?
- What part does culture play in all this?
- What do we do first?
- How do we know we are making a difference?

The tools of the trade include:

- Employee surveys (past and present)

- Surveys of other stakeholders including customers and shareholders

- Comparative studies of competitors or other organisations

- Assessments of stakeholder needs

- Assessments of stakeholder power and influence

- Use of different organisation models to assess current strengths and model new organisational responses

- Conceptual models to assist in visioning the future

- Impact surveys to monitor progress

- Simulations to build and test designs

	Unfreezing	Mobilising	Re-freezing
Analytical tools	• Surveys • Benchmarking	• Vision development • Organisation capability modelling • Change phases • Change programming • Stakeholder assessments	• Review and audit • Learning dissemination • Recognition of history and loss
Engagement Process	• Focus groups • Large scale events	• Steering groups • Change teams • Project groups • Workshops • Large scale events • Training and education	• Education and training • Diagonal slice groups • Using new organisational structures • Business planning and performance review

Table 7

Engagement

To work the analysis into collective insight and commitment to change we might employ a number of different engagement processes:

- Large scale events

- Workshops

- Project sessions

- Focus groups

- Coaching and learning sets

The combination of analytical techniques and engagement processes form the bedrock of change management process to be employed with particular purpose at key stages of the change cycle.

Summary

Most projects ultimately require people to think and behave in a different way and, therefore, project management needs to integrate change management thinking. Change management requires consideration of all the aspects of the envisaged change, which then need to be reflected in the definition of project success. The psychology of change points to predictable reactions to change, and offers the project manager ways to assist individuals in seeing the need for change and playing their part in it. The approach to change management is a choice : senior management must decide what general approach to take. They may be able to command or require support in the short term, but longer term sustainable change requires a greater level of active engagement by staff and other stakeholders working across the organisation or system. There is a range of engagement activities, and they take time to plan and set up. Communications planning and execution is crucial in change environments, but it is more limited in its objectives for ownership of change. An engagement strategy is key in ensuring support and acceptance.

Now it is your turn!

Think of your project and answer the following questions:

1. **What kind of change is your project intended to achieve?**

2. **Who are the key stakeholders and how will they view change?**

3. **What phases of change can you see?**

4. **What general philosophy of change will you adopt?**

5. **What key change management tools and techniques will need to be employed?**

Chapter Eight

Case Study on Change

> The academic leaders and senior hospital doctors got together over the weekend to consider the need to re-design the current 5 year undergraduate medical course. A report from the General Medical Council had already set out the general need for reform, but the details had to be worked on locally. But why did they need to change? There was no shortage of applications to study medicine and the School generally had a good reputation. Nevertheless, a nucleus realised that the demands of medicine were changing and that newly qualified doctors needed to be more skilful, empathetic, patient focussed and less full of science fact. Other schools had already embarked on new programmes and there was a danger that this one might be left behind. Everyone who was there at the weekend conference knew that it would be a difficult change to contemplate, with many established and comfortable teaching routines disrupted by new ideas for content and teaching process.

This case study focuses on change for two organisations (a university and a hospital) working as one within a Medical School to produce doctors. The case looks back over a four year change programme providing a snapshot of issues and a change management process that started with the weekend retreat.

The particular learning points coming from the case are that:

- It can take time to achieve consensus on the case for change

- There is a need to externalise the requirement for change in order to give it real legitimacy and drive

- In cultures that are professional and collegiate but not managerial, much of the change process is informal and rather subtle. Coalitions of the willing and enthusiastic are key, leadership is at a premium

- Vision building needs time and requires broad endorsement

- Programme and project management disciplines help to give structure and momentum

- Phases of change are helpful in providing a motivational escalator for change

- Project team working is essential in providing a counter organisation to mix players and experiment with the future away from the constraints of customary organisation structures

- A careful mix of focussed project working, with large scale group interventions is key to ensuring movement and buy in at the same time

- Good Change Programme governance is essential in building confidence in the decisions that must ultimately be made

- **A Communications Strategy is key to ensuring shift over time in attitudes and behaviour**

We should begin the case by commenting on some distinct cultural issues:

- The two sponsoring organisations had different reasons for existence. The hospital's main purpose was the diagnosis and treatment of ill patients and the university's object was the achievement of learning to degree level and research. The Medical School represented a joint venture with financial flows to recognise and reward the joint commitment. However, given that university teachers and hospital doctors had broader remits than the training of doctors, the change in doctor training would always have to be negotiated against the broader back drop of the sponsor's interests. More importantly the key players at the table would always have a broader identity and allegiance.

- Within the Medical School there was a mix of motivation. Hospital based clinical teaching staff were driven by the desire to produce doctors. University based science saw their role as producing scientists some of whom may choose to be doctors.

- The Medical School brought together professional and collegiate cultures but with some tension. Hospital based staff had become affected by the gradual and increasingly more pervasive management culture within healthcare. The University was much less subject to these values and processes. The tension played out in the degree to which the desired change management process was formalised and driven as opposed to loosely configured and emerging.

- The Medical School itself was relatively untouched by management process. Management information and control systems governing the activity, quality and costs of the curriculum were at the time of this project, embryonic. Quality of education process was audited but there was imprecision in the standards to be achieved. The output measure lay in exam success, but internal value was placed on professional academic freedom to support students in their quest for academic and vocational achievement. These characteristics would have major implications for the scale of change required and degree of resistance to be encountered.

We know from the previous chapter how important it is to have a clear and compelling case for change supported by a coalition of active internal champions.

The purpose of the weekend retreat was to explore the case for change with those who had a formal leadership role. The case was founded on the General Medical Council report and the need to achieve a different kind of learning product in future. But there were two underlying drag factors on change. The first was that the findings and conclusions of the report were not owned locally, and secondly that there was no external market drive requiring change. The School was very successful in attracting good quality candidates.

To further explore the case for change, discussion moved to the definition of the

Doctor as a product of the learning process with an initial specification being used to test the effectiveness of the current curriculum and learning. As you would expect, there were mixed views on current effectiveness and at this stage there was no external perspective on success or failure.

The early champions of change talked of the need for re-shaping the curriculum to achieve the specification. Other participants went along with this in order to hypothesise and speculate on change and to dip their toes in the water. Early integration of scientific learning with practical clinical application might mean a reduction of scientific knowledge in favour of more clinical and non clinical skills development. In terms of learning process, participants concluded that this could mean a change in the way in which doctors and scientists shared teaching. Other changes might flow in terms of teaching locations, learning materials used, the timing of learning and how it was assessed. Underlying this, participants could begin to feel potential, more profound, personal changes in their role, identity, power and influence. For some the changes would be invigorating and motivating offering new opportunities; but for others, changes would be threatening and to be overcome.

One key ingredient of the weekend was a decision to freeze the relative financial allocations to the two organisations for an initial 5 year period after implementation of the new curriculum. This had a very calming effect particularly on the University representatives, allowing them to disengage the fears of changes in funding from other consequences or opportunities seen. They could, therefore, talk more openly and work with ideas "on the table" without having to calculate the impact of any changes that they appeared to embrace, on the funding of their establishment.

The weekend retreat represented a specific change intervention. The process used was a mixture of large group, small group and individual work. Discussion and work focussed on the need for change and the vision for achievement and the implications of change. At this stage, the engagement represented an intellectual pursuit around change without collective emotional commitment its achievement. However, the group did resolve on some immediate action that effectively formed the basis of a phase one change process dedicated to building a stronger and more collective view of the need for change leading to support for a development programme.

There were 4 key pieces of work within the first phase:

1. **Refinement of the specification.** More work on the specification of the end product or Doctor to provide a goal for the change effort

2. **The assessment of the current course in terms of its strengths and weaknesses** with a particular emphasis on surveying graduates and their employers. This was to externalise the need for change

3. **Research on other approaches elsewhere and the active comparison of the schools process.** This was to provide another external drive for change but also to build confidence that change was desirable and obtainable

4. **Development of a project plan** to take forward the findings and conclusions of the first phase. This was to ensure momentum.

A large group event was used to provide feedback on the retreat and to launch the activity. In terms of governance and project arrangements, the following were adopted:

- A large and inclusive steering group acted as sponsors of the activity and provided a representative forum to review outcomes and sign off on process steps

- A smaller core Project Management Team met to design the more detailed process and to manage the political process

- Actual work was undertaken by Administrative staff in the School with the use of some external research capability

This opening phase took approximately one year to complete and culminated in another follow up large group event to consider the findings and in particular to review the proposed project plan.

This plan then took the change programme into a different gear.

The overriding **purpose** of the change project became the "Development of a new kind of Doctor" enshrined by the specification presented and approved by the Steering Group and the staff event. But there were other desired outcomes encompassing the attractiveness of graduates to employers and the reputation and profile of the Medical School.

The shorter term deliverable of the Project was the implementation of the new integrated curriculum to meet the General Medical Council requirements and the product enshrined in the specification. The broader success criteria for the project specified a course that would command the support of academics and senior clinical staff. Issues of timing and cost were not as yet specified.

The fact that the success criteria acknowledged the need for the support of academics and senior clinical staff meant that the subsequent project process would require heavy engagement of staff.

The organisational arrangements changed:

- The Steering Group's role and remit became more formal and it acted as a Court to agree curriculum principles and to assure project progress. Composition was extended to students as well as external expert contributors

- The Project Management Team focussed on issues of project process and overall management and included the key senior level sponsors

- A core Project Group was formed to take forward the detailed work that was now organised on a project team basis. The core team was part time dedicated to the project. Members of the team were also members of specific project teams

- Project teams were organised around systems of the body as well as general skills development and assessment approaches. These project teams were kept relatively small and included representatives from the Basic Science as well as the Clinical Faculties. The remit was to achieve an outline design. The teams were lead by senior individuals who also sat on the steering group

The project teams were then re-organised at the end of the initial design stage, becoming focussed on detailed planning and implementation for each academic year. This would ensure integration of subjects and process.

Looking back over the four years, it is possible to rationalise the process into the key phases that accord with the change management phases outlined in the previous chapter.

- Phase one – Reviewing the current curriculum: unlocking thinking, motivating and getting movement (unfreezing)

- Phase two – The moving on ideas leading to outline course design (mobilising)

- Phase three – The detailed design and modelling (mobilising)

- Phase four – The planning for implementation (mobilising)

- Phase five – Implementation (re-freezing)

Table 8 summarises the phases for their objectives and the tools and techniques used.

The table illustrates a number of important change processes:

- The use of project teams to undertake the detailed work, but also to provide an alternative structure to engage across the system

- The use of large scale events to engage more of the system on key issues and to provide a vehicle for visibly indicating growing support for the new curriculum

- The use of different techniques within each stage to build the case for change, build compelling visions of the future and then move on the detail to ensure practicality and then effective implementation

- The use of consistent and integrated project governance structures to inspire common ownership of the new curriculum

- A programme of formal and informal communications to update people with developments within the project but also to bring staff together from time to time to ensure visible collective embrace of propositions as they emerged

Effective leadership was a key ingredient for success. In the first instance, leaders stuck their necks out promoting a general change based upon intuition and insight that cut across prevailing norms. It was brave. The next challenge was to build a process that opened up the debate to the organisation, whilst at the same time trying to manage development in a focussed and time tight manner. The identification of other leaders was an important element in broadening the platform for development. As the process began to deliver contentious change propositions, the challenge was to persevere with the early vision for a new doctor and see through the turbulence through constant reference to the vision. In communications terms, it was a mix of informal lobbying and cajoling with more formal leadership in the set piece.

Summary

The case is a complex one and is on a scale that may not match many shorter term and more focussed change projects. However, it does illustrate some of the general change management principles for project managers to reflect on and build into their work.

	Phase One	Phase Two	Phase Three	Phase Four	Phase Five
Theme	Assessment of current	Outline Design	Detailed Design	Planning for implementation	Implementation
Change theme	Unfreezing – Building a nucleus and champions for change	Mobilising – Building a vision of change and winning support	Mobilising – Building the detailed vision and winning support	Mobilising – Building ownership and responsibility for making the change	Re-freezing – Moving responsibility for change back to the normal organisation
Change work and processes	• Survey work • Benchmarking • Large scale events	• Design work by body system and skills theme • Workshops • Project groups do most of detailed work	• Design work by curriculum year (1-5) • Workshops • Project groups do most of detailed work	• Planning work by year and by curriculum element • Planning work for functional support • Workshops • Project groups do most of detailed work	• Selection of students • Implementation of new capabilities in readiness for the first intake • Project work now assimilated by department structure
Comm'tions tools	• Survey instrument • Conferences	• Bulletin • Steering group briefings • Dept meetings • Conference	• Bulletin • Steering group briefings • Dept meetings • Conference	• Bulletin • Steering group briefings • Dept meetings • Conference	• Bulletin • Steering group briefings • Conference • Dept meetings
Project formal governance	• Steering group • Project Management Team	• Steering group • Project Management Team • Core project team • Sub project leads • Project teams	• Steering group • Project Management Team • Core project team • Sub project leads • Project teams	• Steering group • Project Management Team • Core project team • Sub project leads • Project teams	• Steering group • Project Management Team • Core project team • Department Heads

Table 8

Chapter Nine

Project Design

How will this chapter help you?

We have talked about project roles and responsibilities and how you move from the big picture project overview into a more detailed work plan. This chapter brings the two elements together in what we call Project Design. The design elements cover the arrangements for leadership and management of project and for how the work gets done. There are always several design options. Our aim in this chapter is to help you consider the most effective arrangements for your project.

We start with some elaboration on the issues we will cover and then, through two case studies, draw out the design considerations and options. We finish by asking you to contemplate what might be right for your project.

What arrangements are we looking at?

For any project, there will be three key design areas relating to the leadership, management and delivery of the project. The issues for each are illustrated in the project pyramid, Diagram 9.

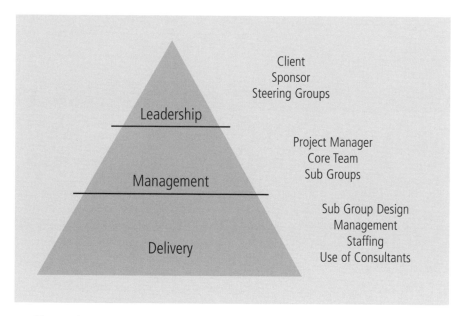

Diagram 9

- **Leadership at the top.** These are the arrangements for ensuring the effective leadership and direction of the project. It is individuals at this level who will integrate the stakeholder requirements and ensure one set of project outcomes and objectives. They are responsible for approving the plan and costs in the first instance and any significant changes thereafter.

- **Leadership and management at an operational level.** Here we get nearer to the actual delivery of the work and our search is for the best arrangements to secure effective planning, monitoring and control of the project, including assurance of quality. A decision will need to be taken how best to organise the work; whether to keep one workstream/group or whether to establish a number of sub project groups with individual terms of reference.

- **Project delivery arrangements.** These are the more detailed arrangements for actually getting the work done. Options may include using an array of sub project teams or other engagement processes including such as workshops, large-scale group events. Use may also be made of established normal organisation groups.

Two case studies

The following case studies illustrate some of the design issues. The first offers a comparatively simple design with minimal overhead and formality. The second is more sophisticated. We hope in this way that you will begin to get a clear sense of the options and the determining factors for design.

Case study 1 – The reduction of costs in corporate legal services

The Situation

The Head of a 50 strong legal services department has been instructed by her boss, the Director of Corporate Services, to achieve a 25% reduction in costs over the next 12 months. These costs include all professional, administrative and support staff within the department, but there is also a significant spend on external legal fees. Management processes within the department are underdeveloped and there is a strong professional culture where value is placed on individual autonomy for professionals and a highly structured and risk adverse approach to the use of administrative and support staff. The key customers for legal services are the commercial divisions of the company, but they do not bear the budget or direct costs of service. There has been a high level of dissatisfaction expressed over the response times from the department. This performance issue is acknowledged, but explained away by pressure of demand for support and overstretch of the more popular legal advisors.

The Project Design

The Project Design for the Corporate Services Project chart, Diagram 10, summarises the key points of the design for this project.

The particular features of this approach are as follows:

- The separation of the client and sponsor role

- The secondment of a commercial manager into the department for the duration of the project to provide project management. This was done on a 2 days per week basis for 3 months

- The creation of a multi-skilled Project Team working on a half time basis for 3 months. The team was comprised of legal services staff supported by an advisor from the company's organisation and methods group (O&M, an internal consultancy group)

- The use of external consultants to support the Project Lead

- The use of workshops at key stages to evaluate current services and to develop/test ideas for change

Design for the corporate legal services project

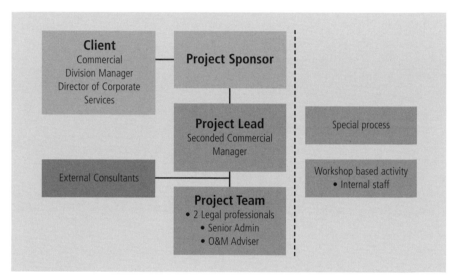

Diagram 10

Case study 2 – Healthcare Services Project

The Situation

The Chief Executive of a healthcare organisation needs to review the organisation's long term strategy in the light of a particularly difficult financial position and emerging major changes to the operating environment with new competitors for some of the portfolio. The current organisation has been formed through the merger of two independent organisations; the merger has been problematic with continuing inconsistency of service process and considerable duplicated costs. The CE is particularly concerned to separate short term fire fighting on costs from a more considered and profound process aimed to build clarity of direction for the service portfolio and the organisation. Directors and senior managers are very stretched and clinical professionals are frustrated and worried. There is a new contingent of Non Executive Directors on the Board.

Project Design

The Project Design for the Healthcare Services Project chart, Diagram Eleven, illustrates key features of the approach, which are as follows:

- The Chief Executive and Non Executive Directors formed a Steering Group to take the internal client role

- The external client perspective was represented by a Chief Executive Group drawn from corporate customers of the organisation

- There was a Senior Project Director working on half time basis to manage the project

- 6 Workstreams were established to focus on specific services and organisational capabilities.

- Each workstream was sponsored by an Executive Director

- Each workstream had a Team Manager and a Lead Professional. The team managers worked on a half time basis with less time committed each week by lead professionals

- A Strategy Team comprised of the 6 workstream Sponsors, Managers and Clinical Leads together with the Project Director to give shape to the activity and to achieve integration of the work to form a corporate strategy. A Service User Group was set up to influence the process and reported to the Strategy Team rather than the Steering Group

- Extensive use was made of current established organisational processes, but with additional commitment to special workshops and conferences

The Project Design for the Healthcare Services Project

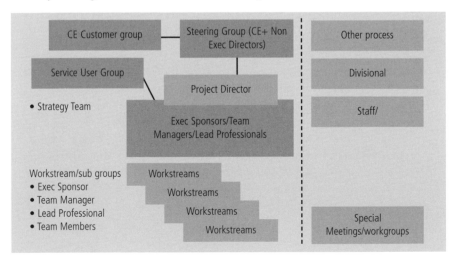

Diagram 11

General considerations in Project Design

There are a number of key issues in approaching the design:

- **The separation of the Client and Sponsor perspectives.** Chapter 3 (Project Roles) emphasised the client role in focussing on what needs to be delivered, or the end product. The Clients may be end users (e.g. users of the new computer system delivered by the project), or they may be taking an implementation responsibility for the next stage of the project (and so becoming suppliers upon handover of the project). The chapter also proposed that where there are a number of interested parties, the client must integrate the needs into one specification. The Sponsor perspective, however, is different. It is oriented to the process of delivering the project. Sponsors, therefore, have more of a "supplier" mentality. Given that there are always trade offs to be had between the user requirement and what can be realistically provided as a solution, it is important to separate the client and customer perspectives.

Where Sponsors also play Clients, there is potential for the supply considerations to dominate what really is required. The customer benefit may be then compromised.

- **Effective involvement of Stakeholders.** The chapter on Change Management emphasised the skill of recognising key stakeholders, their need for their active involvement on the one hand, and judgement about their relevant contribution on the other. Involvement can be achieved in a number of different ways. At a senior level, stakeholders can be positioned as clients or sponsors. A steering group is a way of bringing senior players together. But there are other ways of securing involvement. Stakeholders can be an integral part of the project delivery through participation within project teams. They can be invited to specific activities such as workshops and large scale events. **From a design perspective the important issue is to evaluate how best to involve stakeholders in order to add value to the work and to enable implementation downstream.**

- **Separation of strategy from operational control of the project.** For most projects there are big strategic decisions (on scope, objectives, the plan and resourcing then policy making) and there are on going operational decisions (mainly on getting work done). It is important that different decisions have appropriate levels of management commitment. Therefore, **the design of the project arrangements must enable informed and timely decision making with a clear separation of authorities and responsibilities. Lack of clarity in this area can lead to duplication of discussion and attention that in turn slows down the process.**

- **Appropriate levels of operational management.** A judgement will need to be made on whether to have a Project Director and/or Manager and whether the role is part time or full time. The scale of the work, its complexity and the capability of project staff, will dictate the nature and extent of management direction and control required. Smaller scale projects with clear methodology and good calibre people may require a relatively light project management touch. Larger scale more complex projects with high profile and political risk may require layers of project management (Director and Manager). The aim is to secure sufficient management resource in terms of experience and time to ensure effective direction and control.

- **An appropriate use of project teams.** Intensive work requiring multi-disciplinary skills often benefits from a project team approach. Working apart without regular interaction can detract from the quality of analysis and decision making. Inconsistency in participation can lead to duplication of work as new members struggle to catch up with previous deliberations. Part of the benefit of having a team with regular membership is that there is broader ownership and responsibility for the solutions derived.

- **An appropriate organisation of work into streams.** An important design issue is how to organise or "chunk up" the work. The project Big Picture (see Chapter 4) identifies the major pieces of work to be done. The Detailed Thinking (chapter 5) is more precise. On the basis of the emerging project plan, a judgement will need to be made on whether to establish sub project teams or not. The arguments for doing so will reflect the diversity of the issues being addressed (e.g. services or functions), the scale of resources available to work on the project, and their degree of specialisation; a final consideration will be the overall cost budget for the project and therefore the management overhead that can be afforded.

- **The appropriate time commitment for teamworking (full or part time).** Decisions on the use of full time dedicated project teams (versus part time) will in part be driven by the urgency of a project and the need to complete within a tight deadline. Full time task forces provide real momentum for project work and can offer quicker returns. However, the nature of the work may suggest a part time approach. For example, some project work may be subject to variability of intensity with periods of extreme activity and then downtime as progress is dependent upon other events, decisions or people. A full time approach might mean periods of enforced idleness. There may be other reasons why a full time task force is deemed inappropriate. It can invest too much responsibility and ownership in the project team, and therefore detract from wider notions of involvement and ownership for results. Finally, it may not be possible to second staff into a project full time given the demands of other more regular work.

- **The ability to engage with the rest of the organisation.** For significant change projects there may be strong reasons to keep connected or to engage with the rest of the organisation. This can be to secure understanding, acceptance, or support for the work and conclusions of the project. Small exclusive project teams may have the analytical capacity to make sense of wide spread information and perspective, but their reach will always be limited. Therefore, in the design of projects there is often a need to consider how the project can reach out to established groups and forums and get them involved. It is likely that there are established vehicles for doing this, but there is always a possibility to create temporary structures and processes for such engagement. Special events, workshops and focus groups can orchestrate the involvement of a broader base. It is particularly important, however, to be clear on the purpose of these meetings and the influence they may exert on decision making.

- **The overall cost envelope for the project.** The design solutions addressed above (Steering Groups, Project Teams, use of special events etc.) all have consequences for time and cost. The more elaborate the arrangements the costlier the project becomes in real terms and in opportunity cost (what is foregone in spending time at the project table).

Commentary on the approaches taken in the case studies

The two case studies differ in their scale and complexity. The legal services case is more self contained with a set of internal clients served by a mix of internal and external legal services. The healthcare organisation project is more extensive covering the complete service and organisation portfolio with considerable involvement required of external stakeholders. Given these obvious starting points, we can now consider the approach taken against the key design issues.

Clients and Sponsors

Both cases separate the Clients from the Sponsors. The Director of Corporate Services has partnered a Commercial Head to provide the client perspective. The Head of Legal Services assumes the Sponsor role. Being responsible for the planning and delivery of services gives him a "supplier" affinity. For the Healthcare organisation, the Chief Executive and Non Executive Directors are playing the Client role, but this perspective is enhanced through reference to two external user/customer focussed groups. Given the range of differing external customer requirements, it is important to have an internal interpretation of the priority requirements. This is provided by the Chief Executive and the Non Executive Directors.

Involvement of Stakeholders

Both projects make provision for the involvement of stakeholders via activities such as workshops and large scale events). In case 2 the workstream/sub project organisation creates opportunities for the involvement of certain internal stakeholders in the project teams themselves.

Separation of strategic management from Operational
This is much more relevant in Case 2 given its scope and coverage. The Chief Executive and the Non Executives will approve direction and policy as Clients for the project. The Strategy Team will work up these issues as proposals. Clear separation between the two groups is made easier by the fact that there is little duplication of participation; the only overlap is the Project Director. Strategic issues for the Legal Services case will be dealt with as the Project Sponsor works issues with the two Clients.

Appropriate layers of project management
Case 1 has a project manager providing direction and management for the one project team. Case 2 makes provision for an overall Project Director with team leaders assigned to each of the 6 sub project teams (called workstreams). Clearly, the process management and integration issues are considerably more complex for the second case and justify having a senior level Project Director overseeing the work of sub project managers.

The approach to project team work
Both projects use teams to progress the work, but Case 2 uses a more intricate design with sub project workstreams organised around key service and organisational capabilities. The need for credible analysis as well as broader support for recommendations makes the workstream design an attractive vehicle for engagement. The use of workstreams does, however, require an effective integration of issues by the strategy team. Deficiencies in this process might render the corporate strategy incoherent and not joined up.

Part time or full time managers and teams
Neither case assumes full time project working by managers or team members. In both cases this is in part a reflection of the inability to move staff full time onto projects. However, the work rhythm and flow for both will at times be inconsistent, giving rise to inefficient use of resources if members work on a full time basis. Case 2 assumes a greater degree of internal and external stakeholder engagement. In this approach care will need to be taken to ensure that project team members do not become sole custodians and champions of the eventual strategy. As they engage others outside of the team they may give the impression of involvement, but in reality the process becomes a more closed testing of the team's ideas and proposals.

Engaging with the rest of the organisation
The second case, in particular, strives to link with the normal service organisation and established groups/forums. This will be very important in supporting broader change management objectives as the project moves from strategy formulation to implementation.

Summary

Once the scale of the project is understood it is then possible to design the arrangements for leadership, management and how the work actually gets done. Consideration needs to be given to design at the top, middle and bottom of the project pyramid. The overall determining factors are the scale and complexity of the project and the need for leadership and management at strategic and operational levels. Project teams are a very good way of marshalling resource, but there are a range of alternative processes to use to enable analysis and engagement. Capacity, capability and costs may all be constraining factors.

Now it is your turn!

Think about your project:

1. **What leadership arrangements do you envisage?**

2. **Who will play the Client and Sponsor role? Will you separate this or bring them together?**

3. **Will you use a project team approach and if so how many project teams do you anticipate? What kind of time commitment will be required?**

4. **How much management is required to ensure effective project direction and control?**

5. **What other engagement or involvement processes do you see?**

Chapter Ten

Projects and Teams

How will this chapter help you?

There is something different about project teams. They are formed, achieve their mission and then generally disband. Members have to hit the ground running and there is little time to devote to improving teamwork. If team members are part time, then their prime allegiance will probably be elsewhere in the organisation. All of this makes the task of project team leader rather challenging. This chapter aims to help you maximise team effectiveness over the life of the project. We start with a summary of what is known about teams and then apply this to project work, focussing on particular project phases. We then ask you to consider what you will do in your project to get the best from your team.

What is known about effective teamwork?

There is a wealth of literature and evidence on what makes for effective teamwork. In a nutshell, it seems to boil down to having:

- **Clear objectives and goals**

- **An appropriate mix of skills and expertise and be of an optimum size**

- **Good working process**

- **The potential to meet the needs of team members as well as the organisation**

- **A positive working culture**

Clear objectives

Objective setting is key to clarifying what a team has been established to achieve. Clear and measurable objectives establish common purpose for a team along with a shared understanding of what is reasonable (and unreasonable) to expect in terms of performance. Measurable objectives provide the basis for the recognition of team and individual performance and they help to enforce a team's terms of reference and identity.

Skills and expertise, personal style and team size

The remit of the team should dictate the range of skills and expertise it requires. This may span:

- Functional/technical expertise (operations, finance, personnel, etc.)

- Process experience (downsizing, expansion, reengineering, etc.)

- Networking or political expertise (connections outside of the team with key networks and groups)

- Cultural expertise (cross-institutional, national, international)

Personality and behaviour preferences also influence a team's effectiveness.

We have already referred to the work of Myers and Briggs in assisting our understanding of differences between individuals in terms of their relative preference for:

- *Extroverted* versus *introverted* behaviours

- Detailed information gathering on past and present (*sensing*) versus conceptual and futuristic thinking (*intuition*)

- Analytical and structured decision making (*thinking*) versus value based judgements (*feeling*)

- The preference to close on options (*judging*) or keep them open (*perceiving*)

The work of Meredith Belbin also broadens our view with his model of different roles within a team over and above those assumed by technical and functional expertise. Well functioning teams need a distribution of:

- **Action oriented roles** – the task leadership of the *Shaper*, the practical organising of the *Implementer*, the closure of the *Finisher*

- **People oriented roles** – the social leadership of the *Chairman*, the personal support of the *Team Worker* and the integrative role of the *Resource Investigator*

- **Thinking roles** – the creativity of the *Plant* and the critical appreciation of *Monitor Evaluator*

The essential proposition running through Belbin's work is that a team composed of a mix of skills and preferences is more likely to succeed than those based solely on high intellect and technical expertise.

In terms of size, a team of 6-8 is believed to offer the most effective working solution. Bigger teams can lead to a dilution of contribution, unwieldy dynamics or the crowding out of some players. Above all, the transaction costs of ensuring effective teamwork can outweigh the potential benefit of the wider knowledge and skill base. With a team of fewer than 6, there is a danger that the resource base is too narrow.

Good working processes

Teams need to have effective working processes in order to fulfil their problem solving role. Edgar Schein identifies three key areas of process expertise:

- **Task related processes** focus on getting the job done. These include the basic communication functions of initiating, information seeking, opinion seeking and giving, clarifying, elaborating, summarising and consensus testing.

- **Team building and maintenance processes** are essential to ensuring sound working relationships within a team. Such processes include harmonising, compromising, gatekeeping, encouraging, diagnosing, standard setting and standard testing. The last three are reflecting and learning processes to be employed particularly when teamwork has broken down or is on the verge of doing so.

- **Boundary management** activities are essential to preserving the identity of the team and ensuring effective relationships with others outside of the team. Such processes include boundary defining, scouting, negotiating, translating, guarding, and managing exit and entry.

Kepner and Tregoe stress the importance of groups being clear on the purpose of their discussions when they are together. Groups need to employ different working methods to structure discussions according to whether they are:

- Assessing problems to find the cause (Problem Analysis)

- Making decisions on what to do (Decision Analysis)

- Planning for implementation (Potential Problem Analysis)

These structured and convergent thinking approaches can be complemented by the deployment of more lateral thinking techniques as promoted by management thinkers such as Edward de Bono.

The ability of teams to meet individual needs

The work of psychologists such as Maslow, Herzberg, McCleland and others enhance our understanding of what people need and expect at work with their codification of what motivates and energises (and of course what de-motivates). As a result of their work, we think of the need for:

- Basic supportive working environments (the hygiene factors of pay, comfortable operating environment etc.)

- Safety and security (perceived continuity and absence of fear)

- Sense of belonging and affiliation (feeling part of a group)

- Recognition of individual contribution and development of self worth

- Achievement

- Influence and impact on surroundings

- Development and personal stretch (the ability to grow)

An individual project has the potential to fulfil needs of team members in any one or more of these areas. The degree to which this happens or does not, can impact on degree of individual contribution and commitment.

Positive Cultures

Joining a group or team for the first time can evoke a range of emotions from excitement and enthusiasm to frustration, tension and anxiety. The start of a team often reflects underlying concerns about role, the ability to influence, whether we might be liked and accepted and whether our individual goals and needs will fit with the team's. Uncertainty and anxiety may be hallmarks of the first engagement. These can take the form of scepticism, aggression or resistance, undue submissiveness or just plain detachment.

A team is a micro culture. Individual team members bring their personal energy, talents, preferences, and apprehensions to the task. The team leader creates the environment in which team members settle to the task and foster patterns of communication and behaviour that positively develop the culture of that team. The leader is responsible for cultivating a positive climate for effective team working. Evidence suggests that effective team work is more likely to occur in a climate where:

- Work is conducted in a relaxed mode. There is a balance between structured discussion and decision making, and open more informal dialogue

- There is trust around the table

- Differences are acceptable and constructive disagreement is encouraged

- Individual members take responsibility for moving issues forward

- There is a balance of task and maintenance functions. The team is able to shift from focus on task to examining the effectiveness of the way they are working together

- There is an integral desire to learn and to improve

The team leader will actively

- Encourage individual contribution

- Seek to discover talents in the group

- Ensure that tasks that need to be done are covered

- Recognise and acknowledge strengths and achievements

- Build in mechanisms for learning from mistakes and mishaps and from accomplishments

Summary
In general terms, we can conclude that effective team working will be a function of a keen sense of purpose, an effective mix of expertise and skills, good working processes, a fit of personal expectation and need with the opportunities arising from the group and finally, a positive working environment or culture.

So what is different about Project Teams?
Project teams differ from regular teams in a number of important respects. Firstly, teams are formed and work in an intensive way around a specific purpose. Once they

have achieved this purpose they generally disband. Secondly, team members may well be drawn from across an organisation and have no prior association. Thirdly, team members might be selected on the basis of expertise, but not exclusively so; other factors might well be relevant including the degree to which members represent the organisation system, whether they are available, or the fact that they want to work on the project. Lastly, project teams may work on a full time task force basis, but most are part time.

On the basis of these characteristics, a number of issues arise:

- There may be little time to form and develop their working

- Achievement of project milestones and objectives is likely to dominate other considerations

- The temporary nature of the project organisation may be less conducive to meeting individual team members' psychological needs

- The identity of the team is almost always likely to be subordinate to a team member's team of origin and line management

- There will be active competition for an individual's time between project and non project commitments

For the project manager this is a challenging proposition. But there are a number of strategies that can be employed to impact on team development and performance.

In our approach, we want to consider action that might be taken during each of the key phases of the project:

- The Pre-start up selection of the team

- Start up of the Project

- Performing and delivery phase

- Close out and learning

Pre-start up selection of the Team

"This is a really important project for the organisation", the Project Manager explained to the senior Directors. "Developing a service strategy for the next 3 years is not something we do that often and I need really good people to work on this. There are two key issues in selecting the core group. Firstly, we need to gather potential champions for change in the organisation, people who will be able to implement the changes downstream. We also need to make sure that we have the requisite skill and knowledge around the table to make recommendations credible and to make them stick. This means good knowledge of services combined with strong functional experience within finance, personnel and property. I need team members on a fixed number of days per week and I want to be able to influence their performance assessment at the end of the project so they know that their performance counts. Can you support me on this?"

Developing strategy is a considerable investment for any organisation. For significant change projects like the one above, you might establish a **Core Team** to act as the project hub even if much of the actual development work will take place in sub groups or through contractors (we refer to this in the Project Design chapter). The statement above highlights two key considerations for team selection. The first is around ownership and drive for change, and the second is expertise.

We know from our previous discussion on change, that **ownership and drive for change** are important in giving change momentum, and we also know that there are a number of ways that key personnel and stakeholders can get involved. The Core Project Team can provide an excellent vehicle for this especially if the project is going to take some time and is likely to move from phases of strategy development to implementation. Project teams offer an opportunity for the organisation to experiment with the way work gets done because they can provide a parallel or counter structure removed from the usual line management politics, cultures and tribal norms.

The second point is having the right **expertise** for the job. The first port of call is normally to consider technical or functional knowledge and skill. In the example above, what gets emphasised is service, functional knowledge and experience. But there are other project requirements to do with thinking and communications ability and teamworking.

Team selection will be a function of the need for ownership and the requirements for technical skills, as well as more general skills associated with successful problem solving and implementation. The project manager needs to sit and examine the requirements for each project in the light of the project objectives, the nature of the work to be undertaken and the change issues.

Project Start Up

John, the Project Manager, had just come from his first meeting with the Core Group charged with developing the strategy. He felt that it had been a rather rushed meeting, driven in the main by the project specification that he had written. The team members seemed supportive and there was not much criticism of the proposals. They agreed that they would meet frequently over the next 6 months. They also agreed on a division of labour in terms of preparation of data and propositions between meetings. The plan was clear but John was uneasy. He knew that team members were busy and wondered how they were going to fit this project work into their schedules. He also knew just how different the members were in terms of knowledge of the business and their approach to thinking about the issues. John felt that they would never have enough time together to build a solid common approach and he could see issues being worked and re-worked in and out of the meetings. Even though he hoped that the members might re-group and work again on some of the implementation issues, he wasn't sure that many of them would be able to commit to this, or even that they would want to.

Every project needs a good start up. Leaving aside the need to plan in more detail, project start up meetings have the specific and necessary purpose to generate a common understanding and a critical mass of energy around the work to be done. John's intuition told him that his first meeting had not really met these objectives.

The first meeting of a project may feel a strange affair especially if the project manager does not know team members, or, if the members are not well acquainted. We have already commented on natural uncertainty and anxiety that may be a feature of a first meeting.

The ideal start up meeting needs to provide enough time for the team to get acquainted with the project mission and with each other as team members.

A typical agenda might look like this:

1. **Self introductions.** Members should have the opportunity to talk about how they came to be on the project and their own backgrounds

2. **Sharing information and creating a data base.** This is where members might begin to explore the content of the project; for example:

   a. the context for the project and the purpose

b. the big picture in terms of outcomes, objectives and the major pieces of work

c. overview of the players including clients, sponsors, various stakeholder groups and their interests

d. Sharing information on how the team was put together and criteria for selection (including project manager!)

3. Members' **hopes and concerns** and how they see their **role**

4. Some discussion and consideration of **working methods** in the early stages and how team members might be supported to do their jobs. For example, team members might need additional orientation to the issues, or education and training in particular tools/techniques.

The meeting is working 3 different arenas illustrated by the diagram below, the task arena, the individual and the group.

The best way to undertake the project start up activity is as a workshop or special time out. This offers a more relaxed, informal and at the same time focused setting for early discussions, where there is time to raise questions or concerns.

The team may not have regular meetings as a whole group, but it is important that the start up is undertaken together. This ensures a collective understanding on the context and what is important, with an opportunity to express commitment on the basis of agreed roles and contributions. Trying to make up for a fragmented or incomplete start up meeting once a project is underway is very difficult and usually does not work.

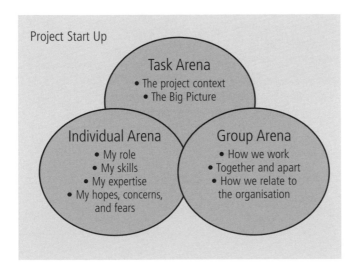

Diagram 12

A vital product of this meeting will be an agreement on how the team will work together when they are together and when they are apart.

For team meetings an initial position should be taken on:

- **How frequently to meet**

- **Where and when to meet**

- **How agendas are shaped**

- **How information should be made available before and during the meeting**

- **Guidelines and ground rules for how the team will operate (underlying principles, what is acceptable and what is not). An important aspect will be the degree of confidentiality observed at meetings.**

Keeping on top of the project is important for all team members, especially in situations where they work part time and may not see each other regularly.

So, a Communications Plan for the team is important in setting out:

- **The regular information that must be shared across the team** (project plans, key products, performance information, individual roles and responsibilities, contact details and availability, schedule for meetings etc.)

- **The approach to the collection and storage of project based information and reports and methods of access.** This may be a physical repository or a virtual library via shared computer drives and intranet facilities.

- **Protocols for the development and sharing of memos and reports**

- **Protocols for e-mail messaging.** Some agreement on levels of priority and expectations of response and the sharing of e-mail (and when this is not necessary!).

- **The role of the team members as "ambassadors" of the project**

All of these things can be revised as the project takes shape.

A final key product from the start up meeting will be the identification of any training and development activity to support members in their role. In the first instance, this is likely to be a programme of education and orientation to help with the content of the project or to understand and be able to apply specific techniques to the project. These might take the form of workshops, seminars, briefings and coaching. Learning can also be achieved less formally through the sharing of information and documentation more informally.

The Project Performing Phase-Reviewing teamwork

It was a busy agenda for the team meeting but John was convinced of the need to review of how they were doing. The project timescales were beginning to slip. Data from line departments was coming through late and he didn't understand why this should be so. He could see that it was having a detrimental impact on the assessment of current activity and costs. Two team meetings had to be postponed because of the inadequacy of data and some of the team members were beginning to give a negative impression of project progress to their line managers. John was sure that there were actions that he needed to take but he also wanted to trigger a group discussion, since team members also had a responsibility to champion the project in their departments and to chase for responses.

We stated early in this chapter that effective teams take time to self monitor how well they work together, reflecting a desire to improve the way in which things are done. Self evaluation of how the team is doing is an integral element of good team working and is vital in securing improved effectiveness. It needs to take place when the team is fully underway, but also early enough to ensure that the fruits of evaluation can be applied as quickly as possible for the benefit of the project.

The obvious starting point is to consider how the project is doing against the stated objectives and milestones. Clients, sponsors and stakeholders will be integral to providing feedback to the team on performance.

Deeper learning is derived as the team explores how their process has contributed to the results achieved. The following areas might prove profitable for learning:

- **Team goals and plans:** How clear and current are the goals and plans? How well informed is the team on goals and performance? Who is reporting on what to whom and how is this done?

- **Team Communications:** When the team is together, who does most of the talking? What does the team discuss and what does it avoid? What roles are being played within the group? What is happening when the team is apart? Who feels best informed or least informed? How do team members stay in contact between meetings?

- **Team decision making** What decisions have been taken recently? How are decisions made? How long does it take to get a clear position? How well are decisions recorded and followed through? Do decisions get re-visited or picked apart?

- **Team working processes** How structured and ordered is business? How long do meetings take? Do team members feel meeting time is used well? How clear is the follow up action? What techniques are being deployed in discussions? Does the team use the right tools and techniques?

- **Team conflict management** How open is the team about differences and conflicts in the team? How much conflict has there been? How is this resolved or not? How does the team deal with differences?

- **Team culture and norms of behaviour** What are the strengths of the team as a whole? What are the weaknesses? How good are they at knowing when to hold firm, or to adapting themselves to work better as a team? What unspoken rules do they follow? How does this behaviour contribute to success?

- **Team composition** What is the team missing in terms of skills and experience to fulfil the terms of reference?

- **Team Leadership** How is leadership distributed in the team? Who is providing what kind of leadership (e.g. task, social, external network management etc.)? How does the team share responsibility? How does the team present the project to people outside the team?

Clients, Sponsors and Stakeholders may have some insight into the working of the team, but such areas are more likely to be within the observation of the team itself. There are a number of options for how the review might most effectively proceed. For example:

- An independent party might interview team members and then facilitate a team review during a special meeting or time out

- A survey instrument could be used to gather views and this could be reviewed at a special meeting (either by the independent party or by the project manager)

Perhaps one of the most effective means to improvements in team performance and project delivery is to refer to the profile of the team in terms of personality type and preferred Belbin roles. This profile might have been undertaken early in the project life, or it could be undertaken during this review. Either way, a team profile can be highly informative, and help individuals understand the underlying factors of fellow team members' behaviour and overall team performance.

Table 9 illustrates the kind of team analysis it is possible to make. It illustrates how dominant types and roles impact on the process of the team, and also how team effectiveness or function can be improved by the use of specific tools and techniques.

Underlying levels of energy and drive often influences team performance. Thus, the Project Manager might want to assess how the project is helping to meet the more personal needs of team members. Table 10 illustrates how projects and the actions of leaders can help or hinder levels of satisfaction.

Aside from periodic evaluations, a useful and quick technique is to end each meeting with a brief evaluation when all present can comment on:

- **What was good and effective about the meeting**
- **What was learned during this meeting (about the project, or about good project team function, or about what to do next on the project)**
- **How the team could work together better at the next meeting**

Project Close out

John reviewed progress with the project team. The first draft of the strategy had gone down well with the Steering Group and it seemed all that was needed was some tidying up. The team had worked hard. Early in the project there had been much opposition by line departments to the strategy work. Data that was necessary to formulate the strategy was hard to come by and often arrived late. Staff members would not engage in wider discussion on performance and possibilities for the future. But the team had persevered and the Steering Group had played their part. There was now genuine excitement amongst the team, but they knew that their role was coming to an end and they would have to hand over their conclusions to the Senior Team for implementation. They would genuinely miss the opportunity of working on something important and at fast pace. A team spirit had evolved and they would miss the professional buzz and camaraderie. Above all, they hoped that the experience they had gained would count for something.

	When you have...	You get...	To improve team effectiveness you need
Myers Briggs	Extrovert, Judging Types	• Much talking by dominant types • Moving swiftly to close on decisions	• Need to build in time to reflect on problems and decisions • Strong chairing to control discussion and ensure everyone gets a chance to contribute
	Introverted Judging types	• Lots of implied thinking • Bullet point thinking but with little elaboration • Swift movement to closure • Use of informal process away from group	• Need for process to make thinking explicit (use of visual aids in meetings, questions to get individuals to express their views make thinking explicit) • Use of questions to encourage elaboration of thinking • Use of techniques to ensure connection with outside world and stakeholder concerns?
	Sensing Thinking types	• Structure and order • Value on objective analytical process • High use of information and data	• Use of lateral thinking to provoke creativity • Development of principles and underlying beliefs to aid decision making • Focus on impact for people
	Intuitive Feeling types	• Looking for ideal solutions • Generation of ideas and possibilities • High concern of impact on others	• Use of rational and systematic decision making processes • Increase emphasis on use of data to test propositions
Belbin Profile	Shapers, Implementers, Finishers	• Task driven discussions • Swift movement to decision • Competitive behaviours	• Process to focus on information gathering and options identification • High profile assertive chairing to provide order and ensure participative process
	Plants, team workers and Resource Investigators	• Support and generation of ideas • Think tank mentality	• Emphasise evaluative processes to gain closure
	Finishers, Implementers and Evaluators	• Emphasis on operational detail • More introspective and loss of connection to outside system	• Emphasis on big picture • Use of systems thinking to draw out connections with others

Table 9

Needs of individuals in teams	Actions that promote motivation	Actions that demotivate
Basic working environment	• Access to good physical office space • Provision of technology and software	• Cramped conditions • Lack of good meeting space • Technology that doesn't work
Security	• Keeping members in touch • Ensuring constructive individual feedback • Inclusion in group discussions	• Holding onto information • Excluding members • Unreasonable demands on time and performance
Belonging	• Ensuring sufficient face to face opportunities • Social time out • Time in meetings for more general discussion • Sensitivity to other work demands	• Being task oriented • Ignoring personal commitments and interests • Emphasising distant working processes (e.g. use of e mail)
Recognition of Achievement	• Feedback on collective and individual performance • Promotion of performance to line managers • Broadening work content	• Minimal feedback on performance • Failure to deal with poor performance issues
Influence and control	• Consultation before decisions are made • Opportunities to present to senior staff/Board	• Reducing individual role and responsibility • Manager taking all opportunities for communication externally
Growth and Development	• Development planning • Opportunities to extend remit and role	• Continued use of expertise outside of the group

Table 10

As projects move towards their conclusion, the shelf life of the team becomes apparent. Members greet this with a mix of emotions. For some it may be relief and a welcome return to "normal" duties; but for others there may be a bit of hole left in terms of the variety of the work and the company of their colleagues.

Recognition and learning are two fundamental components of close out discussions. Having laboured hard and in an intensive way, it is important that collective and individual achievement is recognised and acknowledged.

Recognition

Recognition of team achievement may come from an appraisal of performance by the project clients and sponsors. Appraisals will make reference to the original objectives and success criteria set out in the project proposal, or as up-dated in discussions thereafter. These appraisals may not happen automatically and it may be up to you as project manager to initiate and orchestrate the discussion

Recognition of individual achievement uses as its base line the early agreement of role and responsibility between the team member and the leader. Where this is documented it serves as the basis for objective reflection at the close of the project. As with any appraisal of performance, the discussion needs to focus on what was delivered by the team member. This can be problematic in conditions where the team member may be operating on a part time basis and rather independently from the team manager. This puts a premium on up front and agreed individual work products that can provide the basis for appraisal.

The following questions may be helpful:

- What role did the team member have?

- What did they produce and contribute over the life time of the project?

- What comments can you make about the quality and timeliness of the products?

- What technical skills and knowledge did the team member deploy and what level of expertise was demonstrated?

- What general communication, thinking and management skills did they demonstrate?

- How well did they relate to other team members? What do you observe about the strengths of their contribution whilst working with others?

- What leadership did they demonstrate and how effective was it?

As with all other appraisal discussion this conversation needs to be a two way process and as project manager you will want to ask team members to reflect on your leadership and management of the team:

How effective was your leadership in :

- Negotiating with clients and sponsors on the project delivery and resourcing?

- Ensuring clarity of purpose, plan and direction and in taking key decisions?

- Managing group work when the team was together?

- Managing work and communication outside of team meetings?

These questions should also be considered by your sponsor to facilitate an appraisal by them of your performance and skills.

Learning

These discussions are about ensuring recognition of effort and skill but they are also about learning, that is, conclusions on what has worked and not and what might be developed in future. There are two main arenas for learning; the first is personal and will focus on what team members, including the project manager, learn about themselves that can be put to use in future work. This learning might be about:

- Skills and expertise demonstrated; that is confirmation of strengths already developed prior to the project

- Knowledge and skill that was developed as part of the project work. This could be technical or organisational knowledge, the know how that goes with specific tools and techniques, and skills or expertise demonstrated in the application

- Issues of preference and temperament demonstrated during the project work. This will come from feedback and reflection on behaviour in the team and with the project generally.

A particularly interesting exercise for team members to undertake at the end of the project is to up-date their CV based on the experience of the project and to see their stock of expertise and experience grow as a result. Equally, it may affirm areas for self development over the next period.

The second focus for learning is the organisational one as the team reflects on its experiences in delivering the project, and its interactions and relationships with various sections of the organisation during the process. In organisations where project work is used for bringing in improvement or change, there is real value in the team contemplating what has been learned about setting up and running projects. For example what has been learnt about:

- The role of sponsors, clients and stakeholders

- Necessary support for the disciplines of project planning

- Support for the secondment of staff onto projects

- Successful relationships between project managers/sponsors and line managers

- How project performance should be recognised and rewarded in the organisation

- The wider application of key methodologies employed in the project

Summary

Project teams differ from regular teams in a number of ways making the job of the project team manager a demanding one. Effective team working is a function of having clear goals and objectives, the right team with the right process and energy supported by a positive working climate. It is the job of the project team manager to initiate and orchestrate methods that ensure good group process and balance individual contribution and team interests while maintaining focus on project milestones and delivery objectives. There are a number of practices that can be employed at each stage of the project to establish a platform for effective work and that help the team to build on the strengths of its operation. The process of review may lead to immediate improvement for the project, but it can also lead to individual and organisational learning for application in the longer term.

Now it is your turn!

Think about your project:

1. What key knowledge, skill, experience and expertise do you require in your project team?

2. What other skills/mentalities will you particularly require?

3. How do you see your role in managing and developing teamwork?

4. What practices could you employ to ensure effective teamwork when the team is together?

5. What needs to be done to enable effective teamwork when the team is not together?

Chapter Eleven

Learning from Projects

Most activities or tasks are not one-time events . . .
Whether it's drilling a well or conducting a transaction at a
service station, we do the same things repeatedly. Our
philosophy is fairly simple: Every time we do something
again, we should do it better than the last time.

Sir John Browne
CEO, British Petroleum, 1989-1995

How will this chapter help you?

We wrote this book to help you to manage projects better. We have provided
concepts, structures, and an illustration of skills for you to use as a benchmark for your
learning. Since project managers are in a position to support the learning of others, we
want to close with some ideas on how you might do this.

The close of a project presents the obvious opportunity to take stock of the knowledge
and skills acquired and honed through application during the project. It is also an
opportunity to reflect on good practice and to identify improvements for the future.
There is valuable learning to be gained for individuals and at the team and
organisational levels, but the process of learning is an aspect of project work that is
often neglected. In this chapter we want to focus on the potential for learning and to
provide suggestions on how to set up a learning session. Finally, we ask you some
questions about your project.

What is the point?

The Clients and Sponsors of your project may request a review of lessons learned. If
this is not the case, it is probably down to you. We consider that there is potential for
learning at three levels: for the individual, the team and for the organisation.

The chapter on teams promoted a process of **individual** reflection to establish
personal growth over the life of the project. The close of a project presents an
extremely good opportunity to take stock of knowledge and skill acquired and honed
during the work. It is an opportunity to reflect on personal strengths in terms of
specific skills, general competencies and personal qualities. The learning enables team
members to think about their next job or future personal development. It also enables
a more effective communication to others of growing personal experience and value. A
practical manifestation of this might be the revision of a C.V.

From a **team** perspective, a review of teamwork through the project can help cement
effective working practices for future work. Open discussion of roles members played
and how skills and expertise were brought together, is a valuable recognition of
achievement. It also helps to develop a collective consciousness about what really works.

For an **organisation**, a project can represent a considerable investment of staff time and other resources. Upon completion, the team will have a view on what has been achieved and whether it has been worth the pain and effort. On the basis of their experience, they may be able to generalise on the approach to development work that makes sense for the organisation. They may also have views on whether the organisation is sufficiently project geared in terms of its systems, processes and culture and be able to either make recommendations or actively apply their learning on the next project they contribute to.

Why does the learning aspect of project management seem so difficult?

The notion of a learning organisation is currently very much in vogue. This can be interpreted as a formal programme of education and training where the process of learning is removed from the work scene. We join people like Peter Senge to advocate learning via real time reflection on the job through feedback, audit, evaluation and review of work in action. We see the learning process as integral to the performing of work and not detached. It often means raking over hot coals in the pursuit of new ways of doing things.

Learning may come from reflection on what seems to have worked well and what has not. Both perspectives are challenging, but for different reasons. If things have gone well, there may be insufficient incentive to contemplate learning and change. We may take good performance for granted almost as though it is a natural state requiring no real assessment or analysis.

Some of the best learning will be from when things go wrong. Embracing this kind of learning is not easy. It requires a willingness to confront and learn from what might have been rather difficult moments. It means accepting from the start that there may be other and more effective ways of working. Above all it requires a feeling of self confidence that we are capable of operating differently and that the admission of error is not a weakness.

Just as a Project Manager fosters team work, he or she influences the climate to support team learning. A project team can have a culture of learning where the manager actively encourages:

- **Open feedback**

- **Time for reflection**

- **A fascination for assessing and appreciating what works**

- **Learning from mistakes with the absence of punishment**

- **Communication upwards on the conclusions and recommendations even if they prove uncomfortable reading for the senior team**

• **A connection between learning and personal and organisational application**

Moving from Evaluation to Learning

This book has been about how you establish and run projects. Orthodox Post Project Evaluations focus on whether or not the original terms of reference have been met; they often fail to drill down into the core of the project process to understand quite why things turned out as they did. We wish to move beyond this.

Each of our chapters concentrated on specific characteristics of effective project management. Within these characteristics, we evidenced skills and behaviours required as well as commenting on mentalities and supporting structures and processes.

In the matrix at the end of the chapter, we have taken each of the characteristics and summarised its essence. We then offer some questions designed to elicit learning at the three levels of individual, team and organisation. In this way, we hope that you will begin to draw connections between what was happening in the project by way of process and the results that you actually achieved.

Ideas for setting up a post project Learning session

Here are a number of questions for you to consider in planning for learning session:

• **Purpose.** Who is the "client" for the learning? Is it you, the team members, their line managers or the organisation?

• **Leadership.** Who should lead the learning process? Is there benefit in asking an independent manager, staff member or external consultant to lead the learning process?

• **Place.** Will it be best to get away to a quiet place not associated with the frenzy of the project, or hold the meeting in situ to ensure relevance to the practice of the project?

• **Structure.** Should you keep it informal using simple review questions or follow a more precise and structured assessment?

• **Participation** Whom do you want to include in the session? Should participation be limited to the project team or invite other stakeholders?

• **Format.** What format serves your purpose best? Discussion based on data, formal presentations or brainstorm style exploration, informal dialogue?

• **Outcome** Will you document the output and if so in what form, for what audience and who should record and prepare it?

Feedback on the project's performance and process can be gathered in advance. Information can be quantitative (for example the use of regular project performance data). In recent years such information has been enhanced through use of more qualitative material including observations, stories and anecdotes coming from outside of the team as well as from team members. The information could be gathered by survey instrument or interview and be co-ordinated by an independent third party to facilitate an authentic communication. Alternatively, the questions might be posed in advance of a learning session, but the response handled more spontaneously through discussion within the session itself.

Where feedback is sought, then attention will need to be given to how it will be presented and then used, especially if it includes negative or critical information. It is be important to:

- Feedback the data

- Allow time for emotional reaction (they didn't understand us! they never could have read our communication e mails!)

- Allow time for discussion and to look for meaning

- Then draw conclusions and derive learning

A spirit of openness will be particularly important and this takes us back to the general climate set by the project manager for the learning process.

Two further aspects of process are important. The first relates to the balance of appreciation versus constructive criticism and the second relates to the conclusions and actions that might follow.

For many, learning is prompted by introspection on what has not worked and what therefore has to be done differently. There may be a bias towards the negative and critical and away from the positive. It is important that there is full appreciation of what has worked with full recognition of individual contribution.

For the **individual**, an initial indicator of learning may be found in the acknowledgement of experience within an up-dated C.V., or in the completion of an amended personal development plan. For the **team**, learning may lead to agreement on changing the approach in the next phase of the project. For the **organisation**, learning may be initially recognised through recommendations to change the way in which projects are set up and managed in future. These short term indicators of learning give way over time to the real benefits of learning as good practice is promoted and areas of weakness are improved. For these reasons, Project Managers should feel confident about arguing for some time and a little resource to complete the learning loop.

Summary

The close out of a project is a time for deriving valuable learning for individuals, teams and for the organisation. It's a time to explore good practice and to establish how things might be done differently in future. For individuals the record of individual growth will be in an expanding portfolio of competencies, but learning might suggest further development needs. For teams, learning may help with setting up and running subsequent phases of the project or similar projects in the future. For organisations, it is an opportunity to reflect on what has been achieved and to deliberate best practice to be disseminated. It is also an opportunity to reflect on the degree to which the organisation is really geared to projects as a method for problem solving and implementing new solutions. Learning is a reflective process requiring open minds and the right supporting climate. Time is needed for the process, but it need not be too demanding with a range of options for how the learning is set up and managed.

Characteristic	How good was I (or were We) at...	How good is the organisation...
Outcomes and Objectives **Clear thinking on the reasons for the project and what should be delivered in the long term (outcomes) and short/medium term (objectives and products)** (see Big Picture Chapter and Process Thinking)	• Understanding the context for the project • Separating outcomes from objectives • Clarifying what is in and out of the project • Focussing on the end results and benefits • Being specific about end results, outcomes and objectives	
Big Picture Approach **Clear thinking on the big pieces of work** (Big Picture and Process Thinking)	• Thinking about how to do something rather than rushing into doing it • Thinking and planning at a high level before getting into detail • Thinking about project work as products • Specifying the quality and cost criteria	• Ensuring that business cases are undertaken for project work • Taking the appraisal of the need for a project seriously before projects are commissioned • Valuing and recognising good planning • Devolving authorities and budgets • Recognising the authority of projects over line duties
Detailed Plan **Clear thinking on the detail of activities, resources and timescales** (Detailed Project Planning)	• Getting to the detail • Understanding the relationship between activities • Estimating how long things would take • Being clear on who would do things • Being clear on individual responsibilities	

Characteristic	How good was I (or were We) at...	How good is the organisation...
Risk Assessments **Careful assessment of risks and identification of activities to improve the plan** (Detailed Project Planning)	• Pausing to consider what could go wrong • Giving time to considering the possible causes of problems • Assessing issues to do with the psychology of change • Building into our plan actions to prevent or deal with problems	• Being prepared to invest in preventive and contingent actions
Stakeholder Assessments **Careful assessment of the stakeholders and how best to involve them** (Change Management and Project Design)	• Recognising and understanding stakeholders and their needs • Assessing stakeholders for priority of involvement • Thinking creatively about the range of different processes for involving stakeholders	• Recognising the potential value of stakeholder involvement • Making time and money available for effective engagement of stakeholders
Project Teams **Effective selection, induction and management of team work** (Project Teams)	• Understanding the need for specific skills, expertise and perspective • Establishing good processes for effective teamwork • Recognising individual needs and integrating them with the overall project requirements • Reviewing and evaluating teamwork	• Supporting matrix working • Encouraging time planning systems to support project and line commitments • Having an appraisals system to reflect time on projects • Training and development budgets to support project team and individual development
Leadership and Management **Attention to the leadership and management arrangements for the project** (Project Design and the Challenge of Project Management)	• Distinguishing between the strategic and the operational • Having performance information at different levels to ensure delivery • Establishing schedules of meetings to ensure swift management decision making • Being clear on what decisions need to be taken where and when • Ensuring appropriate levels of authority to support roles and responsibilities	• Understanding the role of Project Sponsorship • Having systems of performance management • Having a culture of devolution of authority • Providing support for the role of Project Managers
Project Organisation **Attention to how to organise the work and selecting the most appropriate commitment to the project management overhead** (Project Design and the Challenge of Project Management)	• Thinking about how to use skills and expertise efficiently • Using a mix of processes to gain contributions • Having clear remits and deliverables when we set up sub project working • Ensuring clear roles including leadership for working at the sub project level	• Actively promoting and championing the project to encourage participation • Financial support for investment in non traditional group working (e.g. workshop activity)
Partnership Working **Partnership working between the Project Manager and the Client and Sponsor** (Project Roles and Client Contracting)	• Clarifying what we were offering to do • Adopting a partnership and peer mentality • Asking and negotiating support from others • Saying no	• Supporting the notion of Clients and Sponsors for projects • Providing training and development to support the roles • Recognising the role and authority of Project Managers

Characteristic	How good was I (or were We) at...	How good is the organisation...
Project Communications **Attention to the planning of communication within the project and outside the project to key stakeholders** (Project Teams)	• Thinking through the audiences and their needs • Establishing a clear communications plan • Adopting a mix of communications methods to suit different needs • Auditing and reviewing the effectiveness of communications (messages and distribution)	• Culture of sharing of information • Technology support for communications • Culture of planning for communications
Learning and Improving **Attention to the quality of the project process and the search for improvement**	• Evaluating the performance and the project process • Looking for feedback from others • Recognising good practice • Learning from mistakes • Planning for improvements • Taking time out to learn • Challenging thinking and practice	• Encouraging learning from mistakes • Recognition and dissemination of good practice • Encouraging time for reflection

Now it is your turn!

Think about your project:

1. What have you learned about yourself over the course of the project in terms of your qualities and temperament and the role that you like to play?

2. What have you learned about your skills and knowledge base?

3. What part of your C.V. needs updating?

4. What does this suggest to you about the jobs or opportunities you should be going for in future?

5. What areas of development would you focus on in future?

6. What information will you gather to aid a reflection by the team on learning from the project?

7. What activities or process would you select to support team learning?

8. What key issues do you think will come out of the project review that will have an organisational flavour?

9. What could you do to ensure that senior management are aware of these issues?

References
and
Reading List

Conventional Project Management

Bentley, Colin (1997). *Prince 2 A Practical Handbook*. Oxford: Butterworth-Heinemann.

Brenner, Richard (2003) *Chaco Canyon for Project Managers and other essays about life in problem solving organizations.* Boston: Fajada Butte Press.

Buttrick, Robert (2000). *The Interactive Project Workout*. New Jersey: Prentice Hall

Frame, J Davidson (1994). *The New Project Management*. San Francisco: Jossey Bass.

Frame, J Davidson (1999). *Project Management Competence*. San Francisco: Jossey Bass.

Laufer, Alexander and Hoffman, Edward J (2000). *Project Management Success Stories*. Chichester: John Wiley and Sons .

Lock, D (1989). *Project Management*. Aldershot, Hampshire: Gower (4th Edition)

Obeng, Eddie (1994). *All Change The Project Leaders Secret Handbook*. Pitman.

Turner, J Rodney (1999). *The Handbook of Project-Based Management Second Edition*. Maidenhead, Berks: McGraw-Hill.

Process Thinking Skills

De Bono, Edward (1970). *Lateral Thinking – a Textbook of Creativity*. London: Wardlock Educational Ltd.

De Bono, Edward (1971). *Lateral Thinking for Management*. London: McGraw Hill.

De Bono, Edward (2000). *Six Thinking Hats*. London: Penguin Books.

Kepner, Charles H and Tregoe, Benjamin B (1965). *The Rational Manager*. Kepner Tregoe.

Kepner, Charles H and Tregoe, Benjamin B (1997). *The New Rational Manager*. Kepner Tregoe.

Longman, Andrew and Mullins, Jim (2005). *The Rational Project Manager*. Hoboken, NJ: John Wiley and Sons Inc.

Pande, Peter S., Neuman, Robert P, and Cavanagh, Roland R (2002). *The Six Sigma Way*. London: McGraw-Hill.

Rasiel, Ethan M (1999). *The McKinsey Way*.
London: McGraw-Hill.

Schein, Edgar H. (1969). *Process Consultation :
Its Role in Organization Development*.
London: Addison-Wesley Publishing Company.

Knight, S. (1998). *NLP at Work: The Difference
That Makes the Difference in Business*.
London: Nicholas Brealey.

Client Contracting

Block, Peter (2000). *Flawless Consulting –
A Guide to Getting Your Expertise Used*.
San Francisco: Jossey Bass / Pfeiffer.

Block, Peter, et. al. (2001). *The Flawless Consulting
Fieldbook & Companion – A Guide to Understanding Your
Expertise*. San Francisco: Jossey Bass / Pfeiffer.

Change Management

Axelrod, Richard H. (2000). *Terms of Engagement –
Changing the Way we Change Organizations*.
San Francisco: Brett-Koehler Publishers, Inc.

Bargar, N.J. and Kirby, L.K. (1995). *The Challenge of Change
in Organizations: Helping Employees Thrive in the New
Frontier*. Palo Alto: Davies-Black.

Beckhard, Richard and Harris, Reuben (1987).
*Organizational Transitions. Managing Complex Change 2nd
Edition*. Reading, MA: Addison-Wesley Publishing Co
(Addison Wesley Organizational Development series).

Beer, M. and Nohria, N. (2000). "Cracking the Code
of Change". Boston: Harvard Business Review,
May – June: Product No. R00301.

Bridges, W. (2002). *Managing Transitions: Making the Most
of Change*. London: Nicholas Brealey.

Bridges, W. (1996). *Transitions: Making Sense of Life's
Changes*. London: Nicholas Brealey.

Briggs Myers, I and Myers, P.B. (1995). *Gifts Differing:
Understanding Personality Type*. Palo Alto: Davies-Black.

Conner, Daryl R. (1998) *Managing at the Speed of Change:
How Resilient Managers Succeed and Prosper Where Others
Fail*. NY: John Wiley & Sons.

Covey, S.R. (1999). *The 7 Habits of Highly Effective People*. New York: Simon & Schuster.

Downey, M. (2001). "Effective Coaching", Texere.

Fritz, R. (1999). *The Path of Least Resistance for Managers*. San Francisco: Berrett-Koehler.

Janov, Jill (1994). *The Inventive Organization – Hope & Daring at Work*. San Francisco: Jossey Bass Publishers.

Kotter, John P. (1990). *A Force for Change – How Leadership Differs from Management*. London: Collier Macmillan Publishers.

Kotter, J.P. (1996). *Leading Change*. Boston: Harvard Business School Press.

Loup, Roland (1993). *A Model that Describes Conditions Necessary for Change*. Ann Arbor, MI: Dannemiller Tyson Associates, Inc.

Quirke, B (2000). *Making the Connections: Using Internal Communication to Turn Strategy Into Action*. Aldershot, Hampshire: Gower.

Sirkin, Harold L., Keenan, Perry, and Jackson, Alan (2005). *The Hard Side of Change Management*. Boston, Harvard Business Review, October: Product No 1916.

Learning in Organisations

Argyris, Chris (1992). *On Organizational Learning*. Oxford: Blackwell Publishers Ltd.

Collison, Chris & Parcell, Geoff (2001). *Learning to Fly – Practical Lessons from one of the World's Leading Knowledge Companies*. Oxford: Capstone Publishing.

Denning, Stephen (2001) *The Springboard: How Storytelling Ignites Action in Knowledge-Era Organisations*. Oxford: Butterworth-Heinemann.

Lewin, K. (1948). *Resolving Social Conflicts: Selected Papers on Group Dynamics*. Edited by G. W. Lewin. NY: Harper & Row.

Lewin, K. (1951). *Field Theory in Social Science: Selected Theoretical Papers*. Edited by D. Cartwright. NY: Harper & Row.

Pedlar, Mike and Aspinwall, Kath (1998). *A Concise Guide to the Learning Organization*. London: Lemos & Crane.

Prokesch, Steven E. (1997) "Unleashing the Power of Learning: An Interview with British Petroleum's John Browne". Boston: Harvard Business Review, September – October: Product No. 4010.

Senge, Peter M. (1990) *The Fifth Discipline – The Art & Practice of The Learning Organization*. New York: Doubleday Currency.

Senge, Peter, et. al. (1995). *The Fifth Discipline Fieldbook – Strategies and Tools for Building a Learning Organization*. London: Nicholas Brealey Publishing.

Biographies

Pat Pegg Jones worked in *SHELL UK's* Organisation Development and Change Unit, and in Management and Organisation Development at Hoffman La Roche in New Jersey, USA. With a Masters degree in Social Anthropology, and extensive experience working with individuals and teams and organisational systems, she has a strong track record of improving performance through significant organisational, cultural and behavioural changes. Her clients include *GlaxoSmithKline*, *World Food Programme*, *NHS*, *DHL*, and *American Express*, amongst others. Pat specialises in consulting to staff groups responsible for implementing change in their organisations, and in developing strategies to increase stakeholder participation and accountability.

Pat is Director of *White Eagle Ltd.*, an international consulting and training organisation based in London.

Simon Standish is a Director of *Change FX* offering change, project management and leadership development consultancy. He has 30 years experience as a corporate manager, external consultant and interim project manager, with a first degree in Economic History and an MBA.

His early career was in the oil industry working for *Esso* and *Phillips Petroleum*. Here he learned the virtues and skills of strong process management. The disciplines of project management and consulting came with his time at *Price Waterhouse* and *Kinsley Lord*. A secondment to the *National Health Service* to project manage the merger of three organisations, fully ignited his passion to work on an interim basis to help secure real change for clients. Simon's clients now include a range of private, public and voluntary sector organisations providing health and well being services. He also has experience as a non executive director of a hospital group.

Index